SAILORS' CRAFTS

SAILORS' CRAFTS

by

Bill Beavis

London
GEORGE ALLEN & UNWIN
Boston   Sydney

First published in Great Britain in 1981

GEORGE ALLEN & UNWIN LTD
40 Museum Street, London WC1A 1LU

© Bill Beavis 1981

British Library Cataloguing in Publication Data

Beavis, Bill
   Sailors' crafts.
   1. Handicraft   2. Seafaring life
   I. Title
   745.5   TT149   80–41249

ISBN 0–04–797004–9

Set in 11 or 13 point Times by Trade Linotype Birmingham and printed in Great Britain by Alden Press Ltd., Oxford, London and Northampton

Contents

List of Illustrations

Introduction

By rights the old wind driven ship should have been an artistic desert. No oils or canvases, no reclining nude, no plasticine, no wood turning lathe, no clay, and no blocks of granite. Yet the sailors in these ships showed remarkable creative ambition, for with nothing but bits and pieces scrounged from the Bosun's Store, working under appalling conditions on mess tables scattered with biscuit crumbs and assailed by flying sauce bottles, the old time sailor would beaver away at his scrimshaw, his fancy ropework, his ship-in-a-bottle, or his carving. From these beginnings an art form was born unique to men of the sea. Befitting their primitive origin these things found no place in museums, private collections or the grand City Halls of those days. More often than not a year's spare time and diligent work would wind up on a harlot's mantlepiece, or be converted into large brown bottles and drunk in quick succession.

Pretentious of me perhaps to devote this book to the memory of these men, especially since it contains such frivolous things as a viewing bucket and an aluminium radar reflector, neither quite within their compass, but if their ghosts don't mind I'd like to.

Acknowledgements

The author wishes to acknowledge the inspiration unwittingly provided by the American artist and writer on sailors' handicrafts Hervey Garrett Smith.

Thanks also to the editors of *Yachting Monthly* and *Sail* for permission to use some of the items originally published in those magazines.

PRACTICAL

Wooden cleats

Whatever other merits the wooden cleat may have it is essentially kind to rope. Look at an old wooden cleat and notice how the rope has scored into the wood, almost as if the rope has fashioned the shape it likes best. No metal casting, however well designed, can compete with that. It is one argument for making your own cleats. Now here is another.

Too often boatbuilders do not equip their craft with cleats of an adequate size. A 5 in cleat designed to hold foresheets which are at least 1 ½ in or 2 ins in circumference is simply not large enough. You might perhaps be able to get a sufficient number of turns on to hold but think of the sharp nips, the constriction and the resulting damage to the rope in so doing. Small or in other ways inadequate cleats can take years off the life of a rope.

Fig. 1   Dimensions and shape of cleat to be sketched onto wood.

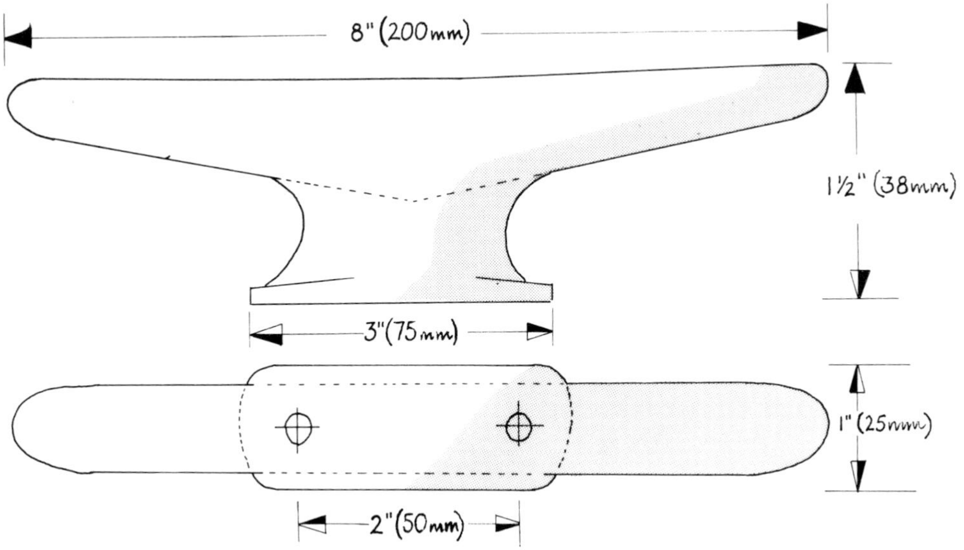

8" (200mm)

1½" (38mm)

3" (75 mm)

1" (25mm)

2" (50mm)

The cleats in these photographs are 8 in long which perfectly suits them for securing sheets. They were made from a piece of oak I found on the beach, though no doubt any close grained hardwood would do. Few tools and little skill is needed to make them; simply transfer the drawing onto the wood and cut out the rough shape with a coping or bow saw. The finishing is done with a rasp (the Surform tools are perfect for this) and a fair amount of sandpapering.

If, before varnishing, you are able to soak or dose them in linseed oil, then this will ensure their preservation. Leave to dry for several days and wipe them over with turps substitute or white spirit before varnishing.

Photo 1   Shaping the cleat (wife posing).

Photo 2   Finished cleats before being appropriated for laundry line.

Wooden blocks

The modern block I believe is tough, durable and maintenance free, but four elm blocks from Thomas Foulkes Ltd, only cost £2 and at that price the merits of the new ones are wasted on me. Besides, why buy new when the old stropped blocks have so much to commend them? Nicely sanded and varnished they look better, are light in weight, have no projections to foul rigging or sheets, are well fendered, and providing you give them a good application of waterproof grease once in a while, are almost silent in operation.

Traditionally tarred hemp was used for the strop since this had the least stretch of all natural fibre ropes and was not inclined to rot. However today hemp is unobtainable and we have to use pre-stretched Terylene which is a hundred times better anyway. The size of rope must correspond to the score in the shell of the block and also the recess in the sail thimble. The strop is an endless piece of rope or *grommet* made from one strand of rope, which must measure more than three times the circumference of block and thimble together. Treat the Terylene rope carefully and do not over twist it or its natural lay will be destroyed. Finish with an overhand knot then cut out half the yarns within each strand and tuck them into the lay. The grommet should be large enough to fit around both block and thimble. The seizing has to be good and tight for not only does it hold the block together but it prevents the pin from dropping out. Last point: make sure you get the block the right way up.

Fig. 2 The completed block shell, seizing and grommet.

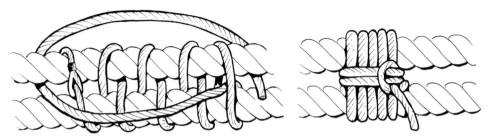

Fig. 3   Rope racking seizing.

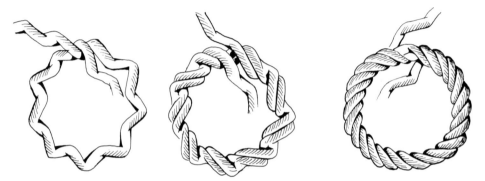

Fig. 4   Rope grommet made from a single strand.

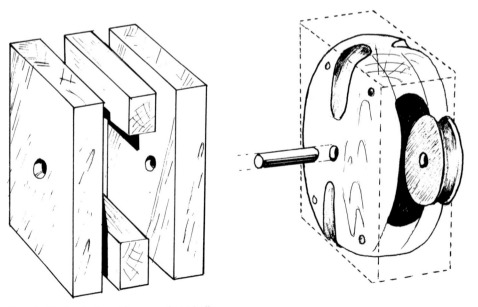

Fig. 5   Method of making wooden shells.

You may prefer to make your own wooden shells and the best way to do this is to fabricate them as shown in the drawings. In Nelson's day they would mortise them from a solid lump of elm, although that method was not entirely satisfactory because the holes would vary slightly in size and a lot of blocks seized up when ropes swelled in wet weather. Sea battles were always a risk in the rain. The problem was finally overcome with the invention of a block making machine which, by the way, was the first known example of mass production. However, back to the present. Use a close-grained hardwood for the job and be wise, buy the sheave and pin (from any large chandler) *before* you finalise the thickness of the sandwich pieces. When dry, shape up with a Surform tool and don't forget that the bottom score, which holds the rope strop in place, is continued right across the bottom of the block which, I can unblushingly tell you, is technically termed the block's 'arse'. Modern glues should be enough to hold the pieces together but you can always add a few copper rivets if you're a belt and braces man.

Photo 3   Elm block shells.

Photo 4   Stropped blocks in use as a kicking strap.

Photo 5   A variation of the stropped block is the tail block.

A custom built pulpit

Galvanised plumber's pipe is a most adaptable and practical material. For the amateur builder, artless and broke, it's a gift from Heaven, for all he needs to fashion a perfect pulpit (or boom gallows, sheet horse, handrails or stanchions) is a length of pipe, a set of flanges and joints, and a forked tree at the bottom of his garden.

The joints, angles and flanges can be bought from a builder's merchants along with the pipe. They include a wide selection of sizes and types that no doubt can be correctly identified by name but for which an outline traced with a finger in the store's counter's dust is usually enough to convey your requirement. They are threaded − some on the inside and some on the outside − and it is this threading which makes the job so delightfully simple. All you have to do to construct the most erotic shape is make a corresponding thread on the items of pipe, which brings us to the only difficult part of the operation and that is to find some plumber who is willing to lend you a stock and die and a good stout vice to hold things. Incidentally, fabricated jobs have a far more pleasing and professional finish than the arthritic looking job in the drawing. (There is more than one traditional builder whose boats are admired for their 'workmanlike' beauty who uses plumber's pipe for guardrails and stanchions.) Furthermore the threaded joints mean that the galvanised covering can be preserved; unlike welded joints where the heat melts the zinc and destroys the protection.

Bending the pipe is a very satisfying activity. It needs to be done, preferably, in the fork of a tree or suitable structure. Apply a gentle pressure and do a little at a time moving the point of bending along progressively. In other words try to avoid kinking the pipe, don't be too ambitious, build up the curve gradually.

Flanges used to bolt the pulpit to the deck will need to be drilled. Remember when drilling steel first go through with a small 'pilot' drill then switch to a slow speed and use a drill bit of the required diameter. The operation is helped by plenty of oil.

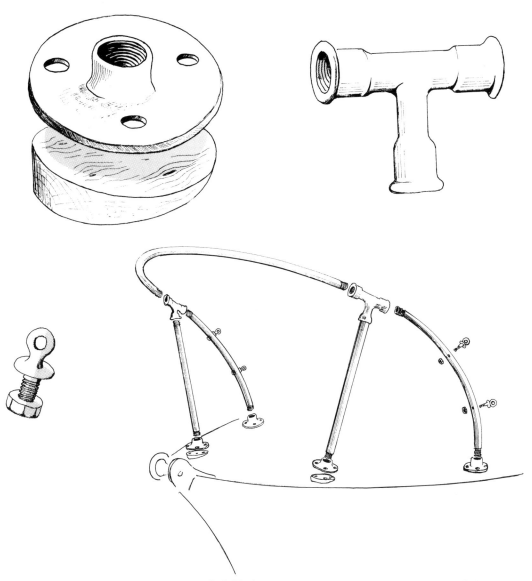

Fig. 6   The pulpit is also composed of 'T' pieces, eye bolts and flanges — the latter will have
to be drilled.

Photo 6   This pulpit was made from 1 in pipe but smaller diameters suitable for smaller boats are available.

One problem is to set the uprights against the camber or sheer of the deck. It may be necessary to 'crank' them to the correct angle with a sleeve of larger section pipe used as a lever. Alternatively tapered wooden pads can be incorporated under the base. The base should be well bedded down in mastic which will also seal the bolt hole where the zinc covering has been destroyed. Use threaded eyebolts to take the guardrail ends.

For additional protection all deck items should be given several coats of zinc rich paint.

Radar reflector

This model can be made in a variety of practical sizes from 8 ins (200 mm) up to 18 ins (450 mm). It is made in aluminium sheet although the construction is much easier to understand if you first make a small-sized paper model. Cut the parts shown in the figure and assemble them in this order: part 1 goes onto part 2; part 3 slides in next and part 4, the locking piece, through the slot marked E which is then bolted at C/C1 and D/D1 to hold everything together.

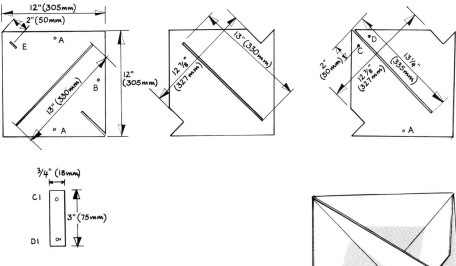

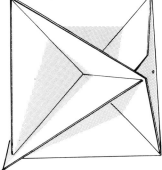

Figs. 7 and 8 The reflector is made in 1.5 mm (1/16 in) aluminium sheet but the mechanics will be much better understood if you build a cardboard model first.

When the reflector is properly assembled, the suspension holes marked B are on adjacent faces of one corner. If a line is rove through each of these and tied to a ring to form a bridle the reflector can be hoisted at the proper tilt so that radar beams strike squarely into the corners. The holes marked A are for guy lines so that it doesn't swing or spin wildly when hoisted aloft on a flag halyard or whatever.

Range finder

Here is a suggestion said to give quick and accurate results. It's a range finder and consists of a 100 mm plastic ruler (transparent for preference) with a small hole bored through the middle and a piece of cord with a loop large enough to pass over the head. The cord is threaded through the hole in the ruler and knotted, and the length adjusted so that when held at arm's length the distance from eyeball to ruler is exactly 600 mm.

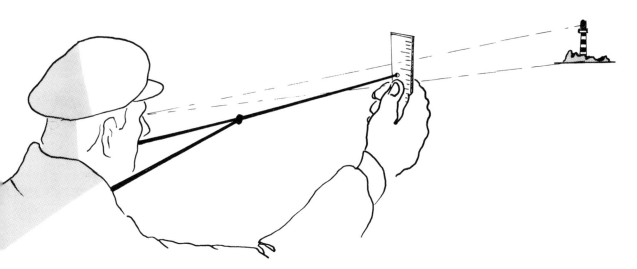

Fig. 9   Remember when checking the height of the lighthouse that it is measured from the HW mark to the centre of the light.

To use the instrument, pass the loop over your head and hold the ruler vertically. The object viewed is then 'measured' from top to base using the thumb to mark base level. This measurement is expressed in *millimetres*.

Then, to compute the distance off, use this formula (a table can be worked out for easy reduction):

$$\frac{\text{Height of object in feet}}{\text{Number of millimetres}} = \text{distance off in cables}$$

or, if it is desired to sail to a position where the vessel is a safe distance off, then:

$$\frac{\text{Height of object in feet}}{\text{distance off in cables}} = \text{number of millimetres}$$

Hand leadline

Any lubberly type can switch the echo-sounder on and know the depth immediately but it takes a seaman's skill to use the hand leadline – a sentiment you would doubtless share had you been on that training cruise with me when one lad twirled the lead around the mast spreader and another shot it down the open forehatch.

Not that such a rustic implement should take the place of the echo sounder; we might as well enjoy the fruits of technology, but a hand leadline is a useful stand-by and is probably more reliable. It also has the advantage that if 'armed', that is to say if tallow or soap is rubbed into the recess in the bottom of the lead, particles of the sea bed will adhere to give some indication of how well the anchor will hold. Alternatively, you can use it to find your position:

'When you get eleven fathoms and an ooze on the lead,
you are a day's sail from Alexandria.'

Herodotus – 5th Century BC

A lead is easily made at home. For a 3 lb sinker, which is adequate for most shallow depths, you will need nearly 4 lbs of scrap lead; waste pipes, electric cable, flashing, car battery plates, toy soldiers, farm animals or chapel roof. Melt your collection in a crucible, aluminium saucepan or a large tin conveniently squeezed into a spout-shape for pouring. Molten lead can be dangerous so be careful, wear adequate clothing and fix up your tin with a long wooden handle. Be warned too against using a receptacle with soldered joints and, to preserve marital harmony, do the smelting with a blow lamp or on a camping stove away from the kitchen.

You will need a sand tray and a quantity of damp sand – *damp*, not wet. The mould is made from plywood and should be 6 ins (152·4 mm) high and measure 1¼ ins (31·75 mm) × 1¼ ins (31·75 mm) at base and ¾ in (19·05 mm) × ¾ in (19·05 mm) at the top. Make the joint edges tight and bind them with aluminium foil as a precaution against leakage. Put a pebble in the sand for the recess in the bottom of the lead and place the mould centrally over it.

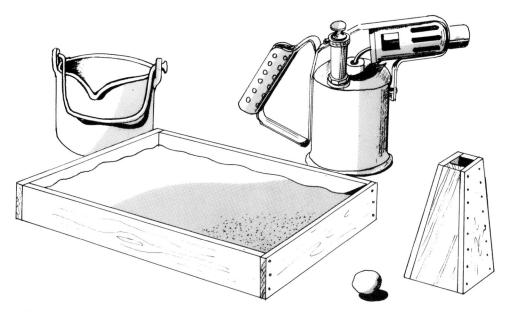

Fig. 10 Sand tray, mould, blow lamp and all important pebble. Wrap the mould in kitchen foil to prevent molten lead squirting out through the joins.

Pour the lead slowly in one operation and allow plenty of time to cool. The creation will have a rough appearance but is soon improved with a file. Hammer the top flat and drill a hole to take the leather becket or shackle. The line can be as long or as short as you wish, it depends upon the area you cruise in. Similarly, the markings may be of your own choice; most small boat owners settle for knots which correspond in number to the depth in fathoms.

Swinging the lead is a satisfying occupation but do remember to secure the inboard end. The third lad on the day I mentioned earlier forgot and ended the exercise prematurely. You could hear the old ship sigh with relief.

Photos 7 and 8 Finished lead filed and hammered.

Chip log

If you're one of those old time skippers who believe that a happy ship is one where the crew is kept busy then you'll love this arrangement. It is the most labour intensive method of calculating the boat's speed man has ever invented, and yet was in everyday use right up to the beginning of this century. When the crew complains you can tell them that. Also, to fire their imagination, tell them that it was from this operation that the word *knot* derives. It is called the chip log and takes its name from the triangular shaped

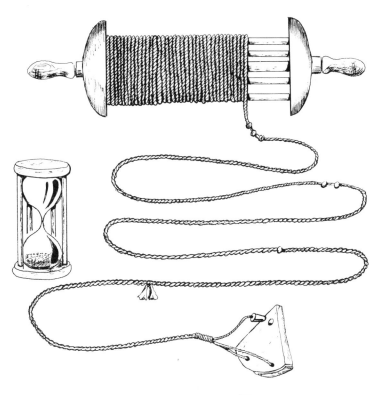

Fig. 11

piece of wood which was used to 'anchor' the end of a line in the water as the ship sailed by. The chip was ballasted and bridled to float upright and the subsequent drag was sufficient to keep it in the same spot − at least for all practical purposes. The line was divided into lengths of 24 ft 4 ins which was as proportionate to the nautical mile (ie 1/240th part) as a 15 second sand glass was proportionate to the hour (again a 1/240th part). Thus the two factors shared the same scale.

To find the ship's speed all that was necessary was to cast the chip overboard, invert the sand glass and see how many 'knots' (the measurements in the line were marked with knots) passed through the operator's hand before the time was up. The number of knots corresponded to the ship's speed.

Notice in the drawing that there are two tails of cloth tied to the line. This was the zero mark and the point at which the sand glass was started. The length between this position and the chip is four fathoms and called the 'stray line'; its purpose was to carry the chip clear of the vessel's wake where eddies would disturb its function. The chip is ballasted with a small strip of lead fixed to its underside and there is a peg in one leg of the bridle which pulls out when the line is given a sharp tug. This operation capsizes the chip and makes it easier to haul aboard. As a concession to modernity you are permitted to use a wristwatch instead of a sand glass.

Teak gratings

Teak gratings are to a boat what carpets and paintings are in a house, i.e. they make the difference between a plain construction, a factory product, and something personal and homely. Yet besides looking good they provide the best non-slip surface you can get. They also keep you out of the wet, never need sweeping, and are supremely comfortable for the feet. Anyone who has ever stood for many hours steering will agree that this is probably the teak gratings' biggest advantage.

Teak is the only acceptable material since it has a natural oil to protect it; all other timbers in this wet and hard environment would eventually rot. However, because teak is also very expensive, you need to take extra special care when measuring up. A hardboard template made to fit the space where

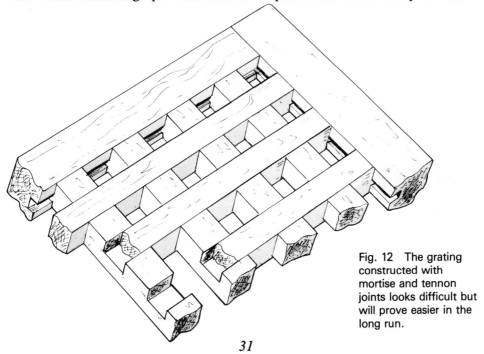

Fig. 12 The grating constructed with mortise and tennon joints looks difficult but will prove easier in the long run.

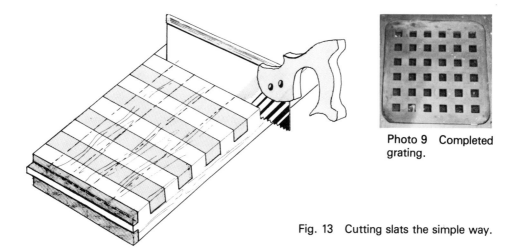

Photo 9 Completed grating.

Fig. 13 Cutting slats the simple way.

the grating is to go will be well worth the trouble of construction. When ordering, remember that the area to fill will be exactly equal to the area of timber you require. Just because the grating is half full of holes it doesn't mean to say that only half the timber area is needed. At the crossover points there are two thicknesses of wood and therefore a good 50 per cent wastage. So, for every foot square of area you will need the same dimension in wood, and at least an inch thick.

The method of making a grating described by the drawing is begun by making a frame with a rebate or channel around its inner side. The pieces of the frame are offered up but not glued until the final stage, after the slats have been added. The slats are made from a solid piece of wood. First mark the grooves which are sawn and chiselled out to a depth equivalent to half the thickness of the wood, then saw down the dotted lines to make the individual slats. (Each slat should have at its end a small tenon cut to fit the rebate on the frame.) This method of cutting the slats from a single block, after first having cut the grooves, is an obvious aid to accuracy. The grating is finally glued together, no pins or screws should be necessary. Neither is it necessary to oil or varnish the wood; besides, sea water and the shuffling of feet will soon leach it out or wear it away.

ROPEWORK

A heaving line

The monkey's fist is the knot traditionally used at the end of a heaving line. Not only does it provide a weight to carry the end of the line farther than it otherwise could go but also gives the recipient something to catch hold of.

Despite its bulk the knot does not have sufficient weight alone and so usually a small stone or wooden ball is worked in to make it heavier. Some sailors use a piece of lead, but that could be lethal. A small wood ball is best. It is heavy enough and has the added advantage of helping the line to float if it is thrown to a person in the water.

The mistake some people make is to throw the line overarm, reasoning, no doubt, that this gives more power, but if the line is thrown in this way the coils cannot unwind freely and very often they overtake the weighted end bringing it to earth prematurely. A heaving line should be thrown underhand, for then the coils come away cleanly and with much more control and accuracy. The range is perhaps not so great but in most cases direction in more important.

The technique is first to coil the line into large bights, at least 2 ft in diameter, then divide the coil in half with the weighted end held in your throwing hand. It can happen that in the excitement of heaving a line the fingers of the non-throwing hand involuntarily close around the coil. To avoid this happening, hold the fingers stiff as if giving a salute. At the same time, though, it is useful to crook the thumb of this hand around the end of the coil, otherwise in the case of a really good throw, it is possible to lose the rope.

Fig. 14 The stance for heaving a line which is divided into two coils.

35

Heaving lines are generally about 10 fathoms in length (20 m). A fathom is said to correspond to the length of your arms outstretched, while a metre in seamen's lore is alleged to be the distance from the tip of your fingers to the tip of your nose.

Heaving lines can be of braided line, Terylene, manilla, sisal or any old thing. The only condition is that they should not exceed an inch in circumference (or 8 mm in diameter) and they should be well 'broken in'. The best way to accelerate this is to stretch the rope between two trees for a couple of weeks.

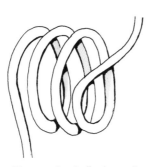

Fig. 15a   The monkey's fist is made close to the end of the rope. Start with three coils about the diameter of your hand span.

Fig. 15b   Next pass three turns around horizontally so that it looks like a globe with three latitudes and three longitudes.

Fig. 15c   The final three turns are made around the second group but set inside the original three turns. The knot is now set up loosely and the wooden ball, weight, or whatever, can be inserted. The job of working the slack out has to be done carefully so that the turns are kept symmetrical. It is best to tighten the knot in two stages, taking most of the looseness out first by hand and then tightening the knot really hard with a marlinespike.

Fig. 15d   To finish the monkey's fist, splice or seize the end to the standing part.

Rope fender

Nothing's so fine and robust as the old sausage-fender. It is durable, inexpensive and not in the least difficult to make. All you need is time. Something like a spell in bed waiting for a bone to knit would do nicely. The fender is composed of three parts: the centre core or bridle; the stuffing; and the outer cover. The bridle is merely a short piece of rope with its ends short-spliced to form a strop and an eye seized in each end.

The stuffing can be a variety of materials. Originally, lengths of old rope were favoured, laid alongside the bridle, and served all together with marline to achieve a cylindrical shape. Nowadays, foam rubber wound tightly round and secured with marline is acceptable. It provides the fender with a good spongy feel and, as long as it is covered with plastic, will remain waterproof and buoyant. Cut and shape the foam either with a knife which has a serrated edge or with a hacksaw blade.

A small rope was used to make the covering in this example but the sensible way is to utilise the strands of a large and worn out hawser: either way it takes about 150 ft (45.75 m) to construct a 2 ft fender.

The covering is put on with *needle hitching* which is a swank name for half-hitches and you do this in two stages starting each time from the centre and working out towards the ends. Pass a turn around the centre, secure with a half-hitch and put on a row of half hitches. When you come to make the second row, these hitches will be fixed to the loops of the first row.

When making joins tuck the ends well under the cover where they will be held secure and arrange it so the next half-hitch sits right on top of the join.

Taper the work towards the ends by omitting a number of half-hitches in each round; the final round should only consist of three or four. Finish off with a Turk's head if you want to be fancy, otherwise just stuff the ends down inside out of sight. (Needle hitching is also described on page 75.)

Photo 10   Centre core.

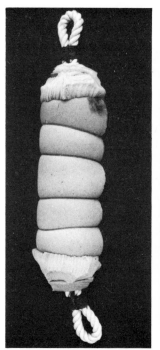

Photo 11   Foam rubber can be used for the stuffing though it should be sealed in polythene to keep out the water.

Photo 12   Begin half-hitching at the centre and work towards the ends.

Photo 13   Half of the fender complete.

Rope fender — an alternative

Figs. 16 and 17 The strands are worked around the hose in a continuous wall knot. To make things easier keep the work fairly open; pause every now and then to work out the slack from below with a marlinespike.

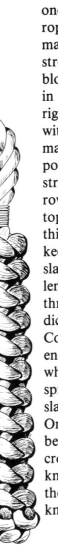

Here is another type of rope fender which is every bit as attractive as the first but very much easier and quicker to make. You need a foot long piece of rubber or plastic garden hose to act as the core and about four fathoms of approximately one inch (8 mm diameter) rope. Middle the rope and make an eye with a good strong seizing (see Wooden blocks). Unlay the strands in both parts of the rope right up to the seizing and with the eye towards you make a wall knot incorporating each of the six strands. Put in two or three rows of wall knots one on top of the other (known in this instance as *walling*) keeping the work fairly slack and then insert the length of garden hose down through the centre as indicated in the drawing. Continue walling until the end of the hose is reached, whereupon, take a marlinespike and work out the slack from the bottom. Once the knots have all been drawn tight make a crown knot (that is a wall knot upside down) and tuck the ends under the final wall knot.

39

A knife lanyard

There's no argument about the convenience of having a knife on a lanyard around your neck; it's safe, you can't lose it and in moments of panic the cord always points to which pocket it's in. Where I think there may be contention is whether it is wise to employ a slip knot. That is the traditional arrangement and for centuries sailors in the Royal Navy have worn this kind of lanyard as part of their dress. The danger, of course, is of accidental self-garotting although come to think of it, you don't read of many who succumbed to the awful threat. However I thought I had better alert you to the peril as I must also to the incaution of wearing the lanyard around your waist *without* a slip knot. The fixed knot here means a risk of losing your trousers. So, conscious of these outcomes I give you the choice, slip knot or fixed, indecency or strangulation.

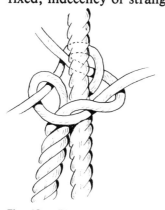 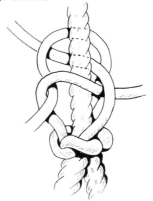

Fig. 18a There are a number of decorative knots which can be used to make the *running* eye or slip knot but perhaps the simplest is the wall and crown knot. Simple because it is so easy to remember — a wall knot is a crown knot upside down (you 'wall' up and 'crown' down). Choose a white Terylene line about 5 mm diameter (⅝ in circ.), unlay about a foot at one end and make a wall knot around the standing part.

Fig. 18b Pull the wall knot snugly tight and make a crown knot above it. The basic construction of the knot is now complete.

Fig. 18c Now taking one end at a time follow round and double, or if you prefer, *treble* the number of turns. The direction to take is indicated quite clearly and this doubling process should not present any problem. When the required number of turns has been taken work the slack out of the knot by pulling each strand tight with the point of a sail needle. Cut the ends off as close to the knot as possible.

Eye Splice: Begin by selecting the middle strand and tuck this under one strand on the standing part against the lay; they should appear to form an 'X'. Next take the strand immediately to the left of the middle strand and tuck this as indicated. Turn the work over and tuck the final strand. The three strands should now emerge progressively from beneath three strands on the standing part.

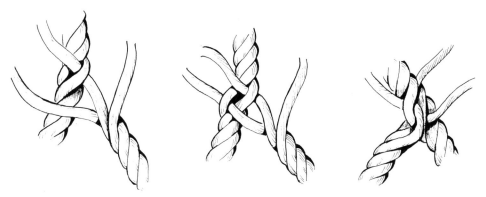

Fig. 19 a, b, c   To make a fixed eye the knot is anchored with the preliminary first round of tucks of an eye splice. One tuck is quite sufficient to hold it secure and more easily hidden under the wall and crown knot.

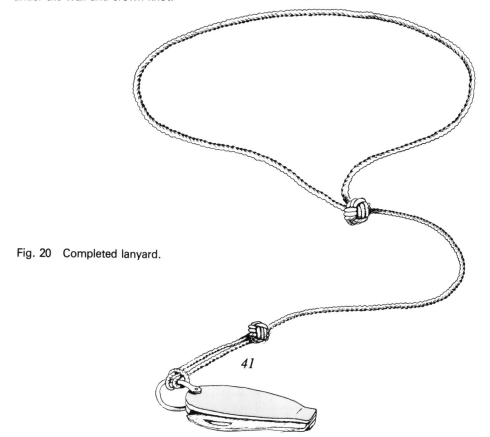

Fig. 20   Completed lanyard.

Pilot ladder

Pilot ladders are distinct from Jacob's ladders in that they have flat treads. The latter are fine for climbing when freely suspended but almost impossible to scale when laid against a vessel's side. It was for this job that the pilot ladder was constructed. In small boats they are generally used as boarding ladders. The rope variety shown here is not difficult to make, is many times cheaper than the factory item and much easier to stow.

The treads are made from a close grained hardwood such as ash, oak or better still teak. They should be the absolute minimum width, say about 2 ins (50 mm), otherwise they will tend to dislodge, no matter how securely they are seized. The holes should be bored well clear of the ends and edges as a precaution against splitting the wood. Rope seizings are used to secure the treads and the method of applying these is described in the item on *Wooden Blocks*.

Fig. 21 This ladder has the rope ends short-spliced together inside a sleeve of lead piping. The weight of the lead pipe holds the bottom treads under water and acts as a step in itself.

Bosun's chair

To a new generation a Bosun's chair describes a canvas arrangement that grips like a surgical corset and has pockets around the sides. No doubt these are admirable and we all mean to buy one some day, but meanwhile, until you get around to it, why not make one in the traditional style? At least you will *have* one when that emergency crops up and who knows, you might even form an attachment?

The seat should be made of good sound wood, about 1 in (25 mm) thick, 10 ins (254 mm) wide and 22 ins (558 mm) in length as an average size. Bore four holes to suit the diameter of rope and pass the bridle through as suggested by the drawing; it is important that the rope crosses underneath so that, should the plank ever break, you will still be held secure by a rope sling. After adjusting the bights and making sure that they are large enough to step into (the top will need to come level with the lower part of your chest), join the two ends together beneath with a short splice. A seizing is put on the bight of the bridles to form an 'eye' and another put around the two parts of rope at the cross

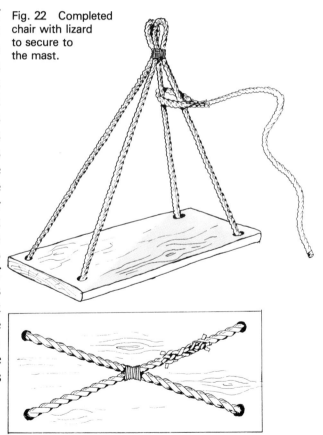

Fig. 22 Completed chair with lizard to secure to the mast.

Fig. 23 It is important that the bridle should cross underneath. Ends are joined with a short splice.

43

over point. A further refinement is a short 'lizard' eye-spliced to the bridle. This length of rope is to secure the chair to the mast.

Photo 14 This picture shows the short splice and seizing at the rope's cross over point beneath the chair.

Net making

Fig. 24 The net is begun with a series of clove hitches using something like a short length of an old oar loom to keep the loops evenly spaced; it is more soporific if you use a shuttle or netting needle. Once the first row of loops have been made tie the second row to these with a sheet bend. If you need to 'taper' the work, as when making a crab pot or bag for example, it is suggested that every third or fourth knot is tied through two adjacent loops instead of one.

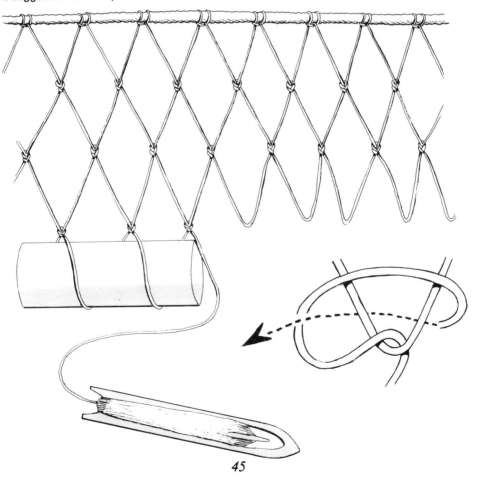

There isn't much you can say to inspire a man to go out and make himself a net. A mindless operation, the kind of old country craft where it wouldn't surprise you to learn that the workers lived longer than tortoises. Still, in modern parlance, it is therapeutic, relaxing and, who knows, probably the country's entire intelligentsia are prolific spare time net makers. In a boat, nets have a few useful employments, particularly for stowage and child control where the infant is caged safely into a settee berth, thus transforming it into a play-pen or cot. Another common use is as a safety barrier around the deck edge. Nets are also good out-of-the-way racks under deckheads, 'pullmans' they were once called.

Photo 15 Netting in use as a safety barrier round the foredeck.

Fish net hammock

The big advantage of the fish net hammock is that you can run indoors in a thunderstorm and know it is always dry to leap back into when the sun comes out again. This is in contrast to the canvas variety which fills up like a baptismal font − quite apart from the increase in weight which threatens to uproot the apple trees. Net hammocks are also good in a boat, useful as an occasional berth and when stowed take up no space at all.

Fig. 25   The completed hammock.

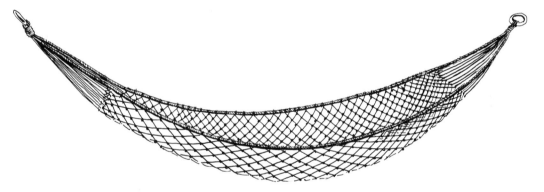

At each end of the hammock there is a clew and to make these you need two steel rings. They can be cannibalised from those items they sell for tethering small animals if no other source is to be found. Put the ring in a vice and drive a nail into the bench about 2 ft away. Now take a length of thin cord and pass a number of turns round the nail and through the ring so that you end up with twelve loops each 2 ft long. Repeat the process for the other end. You will now need a much thicker rope about 24 ft long for the edging. Pass this through both rings and short splice the ends together. A serving holds the loops and the reinforcing rope at the clew as shown in the drawing.

47

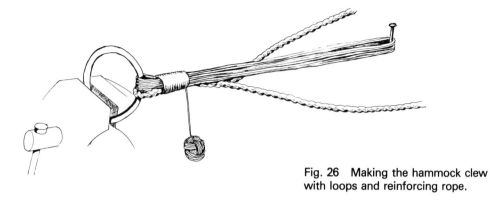

Fig. 26   Making the hammock clew
with loops and reinforcing rope.

The meshing is begun along the row of loops in the manner shown in *Net Making*. Make the meshes a good size and at the end of each row secure to the reinforcing rope with a clove hitch. To shape the hammock it will be necessary to increase and reduce the number of meshes.

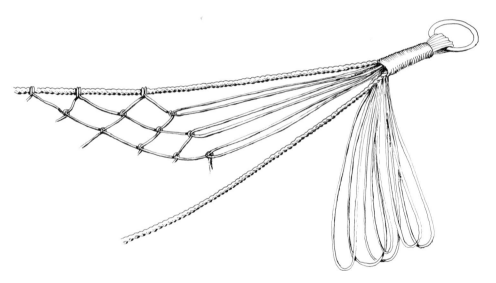

Fig. 27   Although the first row of meshing takes in every loop only three loops have been meshed in the drawing for the sake of clarity.

Rope mats

Rope mats have many uses; on deck they prevent sand and dirt coming aboard from the soles of shoes; in the cockpit they provide a sure footing for the helmsman and won't slip even when wet; at the foot of the companionway ladder they soften and silence the heaviest and clumsiest falls while absorbing drips from boots and oilskins. Finally, because things nautical are in vogue, a rope mat looks good and enviable outside your front door.

You need about 12 fathoms of rope for a six-stranded mat. It doesn't have to be a continuous length of rope since it is a simple matter to join another length by sewing the ends together beneath one of the scallops.

To make the knot, follow the diagrams carefully. Keep the knot flat and symmetrical as you work, and large enough so that the pattern does not become 'lost'. Be sure to maintain the strict 'under and over' sequence.

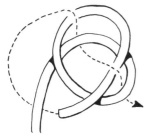 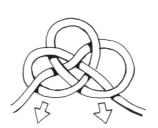 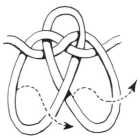

Fig. 28a Form two small loops in the centre of the rope and pass one end through in the direction of the dotted line.

Fig. 28b Shape the knots as shown here and begin to enlarge the two lower bights by pulling through more slack.

Fig. 28c The knots should now look like this with the lower bights proportionally large. Take a bight in each hand and twist them both a half turn in a clockwise direction.

49

Figures 28d and 28e   The right-hand bight is now lifted and placed on top of the bight on the left-hand side as shown in Fig. 28e. (It helps to keep the sequence clear if the bights are given an 'oblong' shape.)

Fig. 28f   With the bights crossed, pass the two ends in the direction of the dotted lines, taking care not to disturb the 'pattern' of the knots as you work.

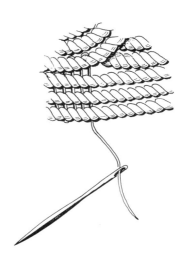

Fig. 29   At this stage the knot is virtually complete except for the job of increasing the number of strands; 3, 4, 5 or even 6 times, as you wish. Observe the strict 'under and over' sequence and keep the knot loose while you are working. When all slack is finally taken out and the mat looks symmetrical, hide the ends underneath and stitch them to a neighbouring strand.

Fig. 30   The sail twine passes under one strand only when stitching on a rope border.

Once the basic shape of the knot has been formed, the process of increasing the number of strands begins. Make sure that they are kept parallel with no cross overs. It seems a complex process, but don't worry — a kind of remorseless instinct guides you through. Your hands do the work automatically; just make sure you don't get up in the middle to answer the phone.

Photo 16   The six-part *companionway* mat.

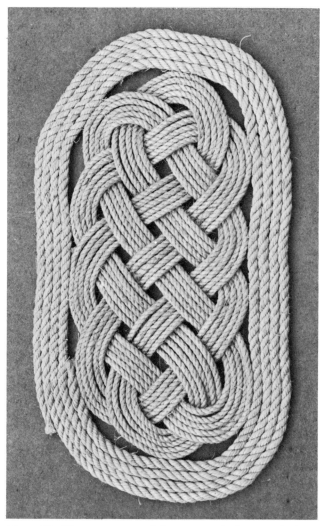

Photo 17　The appearance of the mat may be improved with a border. The rope parts (which can be many more than shown) will have to be stitched together. (See Figure 29)

MODELS

Half model

The prerequisite of an accurate half model is a set of lines drawings, but most designers keep a jealous hold on these and you may, if yours is a modern class boat, have to settle for the lines of something more ancient – unless perhaps you have a very good eye or are easily satisfied. Half models, which incidentally were used instead of plans in many yards and provided the data for the full size model, were traditionally built in hardwood and varnished so that each waterline was clearly visible. However the modern, and in many ways more attractive approach, is to build in softwood which is easier to work and paint with the left-overs from fitting out so that the model is shown in her big sister's clothes. It is then mounted on a blackboard covered with green felt and hung over the fireplace to become a receptacle for hairgrips and dental appointment cards.

The model is made sandwich fashion with planks of timber equal in thickness to the 'waterlines' on the plan. However, if the distances on the drawing are unworkably small then make each plank *two* waterlines. The outline shape of each sandwich piece is marked by placing the drawing over the wood and either tracing the line with the aid of a piece of carbon paper, or pricking through the drawing with a pin and joining up the pin-pricks with the help of a flexible batten or steel ruler. The shapes are then cut out with a coping saw and very carefully planed or spokeshaved to the line. Mark a datum line somewhere on the outside edge of each piece and, lest there should be any confusion, also indicate the bow or stern. If the boat has a noticeable sheer, as the example in the photograph, then in addition to the waterline section you will need to make shorter wedge-shaped pieces to accommodate the rise at bow and stern. Next glue all the pieces together and when cured mark out the sheerline on the back of the model using a piece of paper or card as a template.

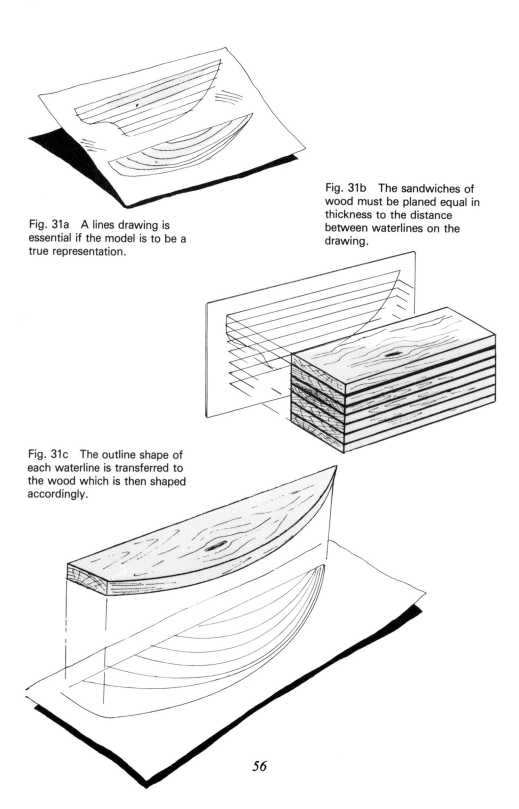

Fig. 31a   A lines drawing is essential if the model is to be a true representation.

Fig. 31b   The sandwiches of wood must be planed equal in thickness to the distance between waterlines on the drawing.

Fig. 31c   The outline shape of each waterline is transferred to the wood which is then shaped accordingly.

56

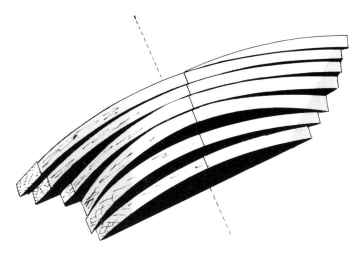

Fig. 31d   Each sandwich piece is marked bow and stern and given a datum mark (in this case running through the centre). This ensures they are glued in the correct position.

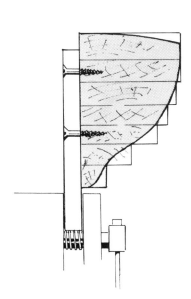

Fig. 31e   A temporary board is screwed to the back of the model so that it can be held securely in a vice.

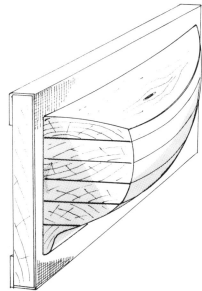

Fig. 31f   The model is finally mounted on a blackboard covered with felt or green hessian.

To fair the hull, screw a temporary holding block on the back which will enable it to be held securely in a vice. Remove the surplus wood carefully with a chisel, Surform tool and gouge and make frequent checks with the drawing to see that you are following each curve and hollow correctly. Sandpaper smooth, using a sanding block as much as possible in preference to your hand. You will need to take a lot of trouble with the painting since blemishes and brush marks are unacceptable in such a small model. Frequent coats and systematic sanding with 'wet and dry' between each coat is the only way to build up a perfect finish.

Rudders, drop keels, skegs, even the base of very thin keels, are best made separately from pieces of plywood glued to the backboard. Bulwarks, deckhouses, cockpit and fittings are not essential and were never a traditional part of the half model although if you have the time and patience they look good and provide a much safer resting place for hairgrips, and dental appointments, etc.

Photo 18   A completed half model of *Dame Fortune.*

Ship in a bottle

Don't let diffidence put you off, the ship in a bottle doesn't necessarily have to be an intricately rigged *Cutty Sark*, it could just as easily be a Soling or a Sailfish, your own boat in fact, and still look equally attractive. Choose a model to match your skills and forget about tradition. However, you can be adventurous with your choice of bottle. There is an exotic collection of glass containers nowadays — most of them more exciting than their contents. I once put a ship in a 40 watt light bulb, then dropped it the following day.

Whatever rig or container you choose there are a number of basic steps and the first one is shaping the hull. Ideally this should be carved from softwood — not balsa. Choose a suitable blemish free chunk, cut roughly to size but twice as deep as you need. The bottom half allows it to be held securely in a vice. Cut the fore and aft shape then concentrate on sheer line and bulwarks — if she is to have them. Carve bow and stern next, sandpaper and cut off the holding part of the block just below the waterline. The hull can be painted at this stage. If you want cove lines, boot-topping, or even lines of gun ports, it is recommended you use appropriate coloured thread glued to the hull. It is impossible to paint such consistently thin lines by hand. If your model is to have deck houses, hatches etc. then now is the time to add them.

Cocktail sticks make good spars although if found too large their diameters can be reduced or tapered by putting them in the chuck of an electric drill and holding them against a sheet of fine sandpaper. For drilling holes in spars a good slender drill bit can be made from a needle broken in half with angled flats filed on three sides. Very fine thread is used for stays and shrouds and to make them more authentic, and much easier to work, the thread should first be varnished. Some old shellbacks swear by nail varnish because, apart from a very high quality finish and good adhesive properties, it comes supplied with a dandy little brush.

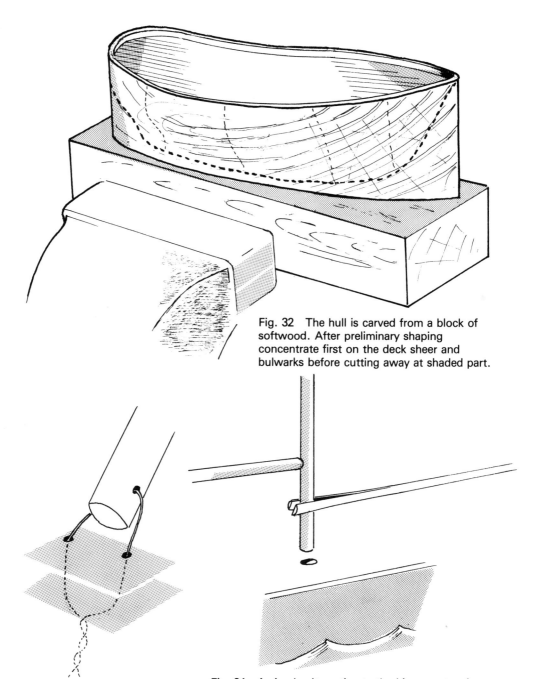

Fig. 32   The hull is carved from a block of softwood. After preliminary shaping concentrate first on the deck sheer and bulwarks before cutting away at shaded part.

Fig. 33   Method of hinging masts with short length of fuse wire.

Fig. 34   A simple alternative to the hinge system is to step each mast separately (complete with sails) into predrilled holes in the deck. Note the mast is held in a split cane.

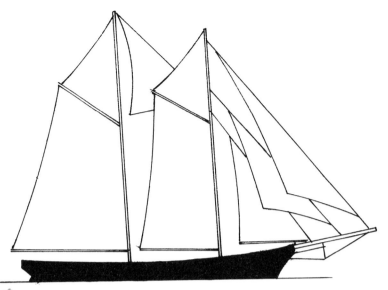

Fig. 35   A fore and aft schooner rig is a good choice for a first attempt and to many eyes looks better than the fussy square rigger. Perhaps one square sail on the foremast to make her a topsail schooner?

Fig.37   Sails are glued with varnish to gaffs or yards only, this allows the rig to be folded flat. For better adhesion foresails are made from doubled pieces.

Fig. 36   Sails are cut from good quality paper and varnished or painted with a water based paint. Seams and reef points are drawn in with a sharp pencil.

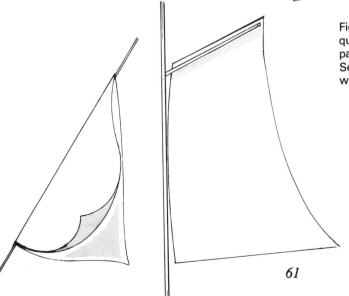

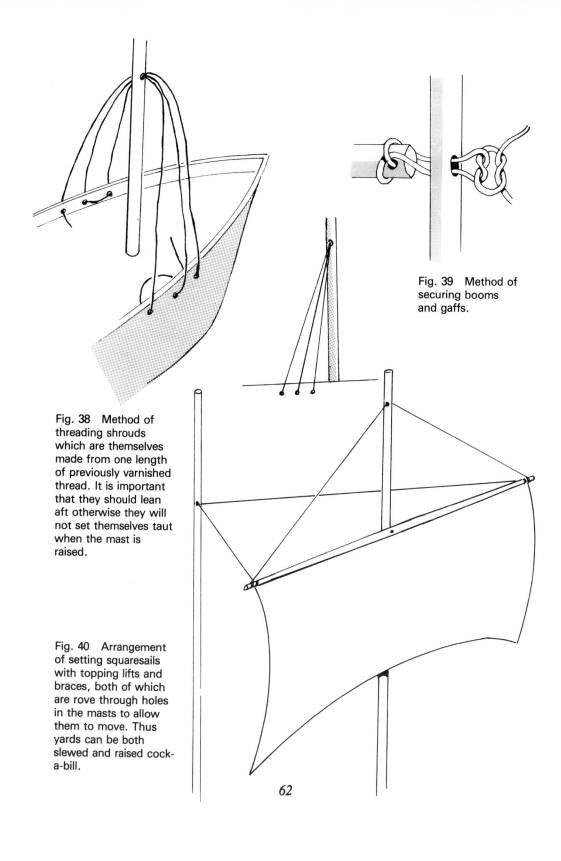

Fig. 39 Method of securing booms and gaffs.

Fig. 38 Method of threading shrouds which are themselves made from one length of previously varnished thread. It is important that they should lean aft otherwise they will not set themselves taut when the mast is raised.

Fig. 40 Arrangement of setting squaresails with topping lifts and braces, both of which are rove through holes in the masts to allow them to move. Thus yards can be both slewed and raised cock-a-bill.

Fig. 41 Useful cutting tool.

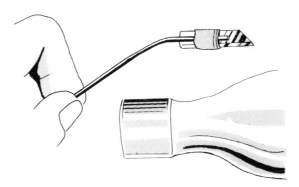

Fig. 42 Rig ready for lifting.

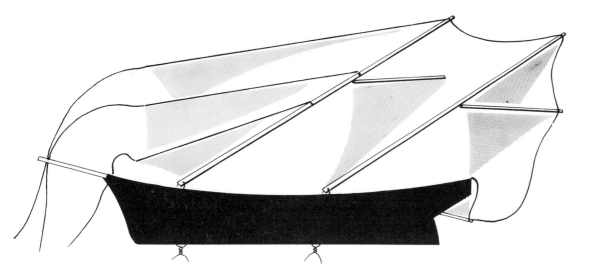

The 'sea' is made with linseed oil putty mixed with Prussian Blue artists' oil paint. Make a good deep blue mix to contrast with the white horses, bow wave and wake, all of which will have to be painted on with a brush. Make sure you have sufficient depth of putty so that waves can be moulded satisfactorily without the bottom of the glass showing through and also, before the putty hardens, mould a bed for the ship. You will need to fashion some long handled tools for these jobs.

Before inserting the ship into the bottle it will be necessary to spread some glue over the bed where she is to sit. To get the ship through the neck, hinge back the masts and gently fold the sails so that they envelop the hull. The final positioning is done with a long pair of tweezers. Press the ship into her bed with a bent piece of wire and, at the same time, raise the masts by pulling on the forestay, or if you prefer, step each mast separately with a split cane as shown in the drawing. Cut off the excess rigging, give the boat a slight heel to leeward, re-insert the cap and apart from a stand and card giving the boat's name, the job is complete.

Photo 19   A small, modern sloop in a bottle.

Egg box model

This display was devised by a talented Welsh Sikh Mr Mohan Singh and was first published in *Yachting Monthly*. Mr Singh had designed a boat and wanted to see what it would look like before tackling the actual construction. To this end he was more than successful because, as he discovered, a model of this complexion gives a much better picture of curve and shape than even the full size item. It also has a pleasing quality of its own. The kind of thing you might like to colour and hang from your bedroom ceiling.

You need a set of line drawings photo-reduced to an acceptable size which then have to be transferred to stiff paper or card either by pricking through the outline with a pin or by using carbon paper and tracing them. Draw and number all the station frames and mark on them the deck centreline, the keel and the waterlines which you choose to use. Two waterlines are sufficient. The profile of the boat is next drawn with the station frame points marked on it. The centre of the profile will have to be removed so an inner perimeter line is also drawn an inch or so in from the edges.

Cut out the profile and notice that this is temporarily out right through at the stem and stern to make later assembly possible. As this will be the backbone of the model Mr Singh recommends that it should be made double thickness, in other words two sections cut out and glued together. If this suggestion is followed remember to allow for the extra thickness when cutting out the assembly slots on the station frames. Incidentally all slots should be cut out with a modeller's knife to give a good right-angle cut (a sloping cut can induce a twist in the model). Once the station frames, waterlines and profile have all been cut out the next job is to mark the stem and keel piece. Select a longish strip of paper as a template and lay this around the keel and stem of the profile; use a couple of pins to fix it in position. Mark onto this paper the positions of the station frames and also the overall length. Now with a pair of dividers or compasses measure the keel width of each station frame and transfer these measurements to the template.

This should now suggest the true outline shape of the keel piece which is cut out and transferred to the stiff paper or card.

To assemble the model take the keel section of the profile and sit all the station frames into it. Now pick up one half of the lower waterline (you did notice these were cut in half didn't you?) and slot it into position down one side of the frames. Next fix the other half followed by the waterline above, and so on until the upper half of the profile is finally slotted home. Do take care with this slotting business, don't force things, and make sure each slot is properly lined up. The last construction job is to glue on the keel and stem piece and also two small strips of paper over the cuts in the profile to lock the model together. Finally there is the job of painting the model, unless you were smart and made it with coloured cardboard.

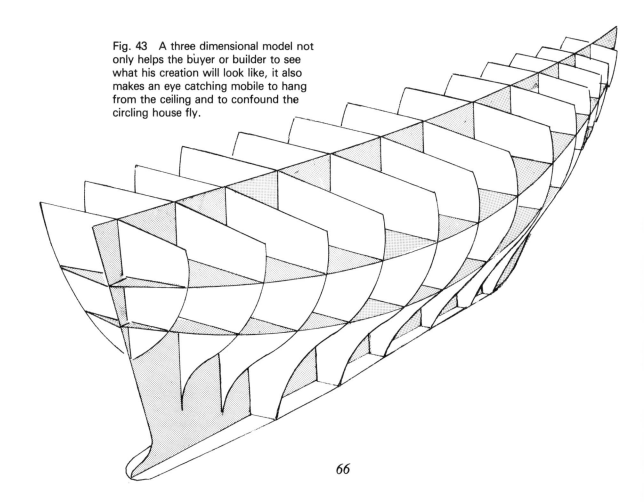

Fig. 43 A three dimensional model not only helps the buyer or builder to see what his creation will look like, it also makes an eye catching mobile to hang from the ceiling and to confound the circling house fly.

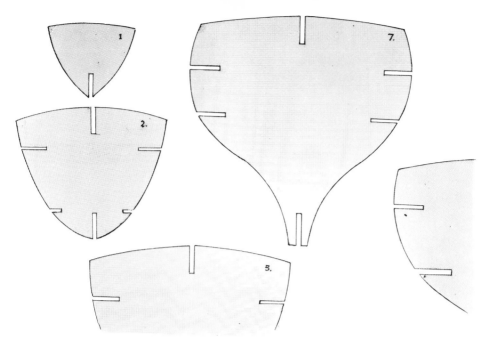

Fig. 44   The station frames are cut from stiff card, slotted and numbered.

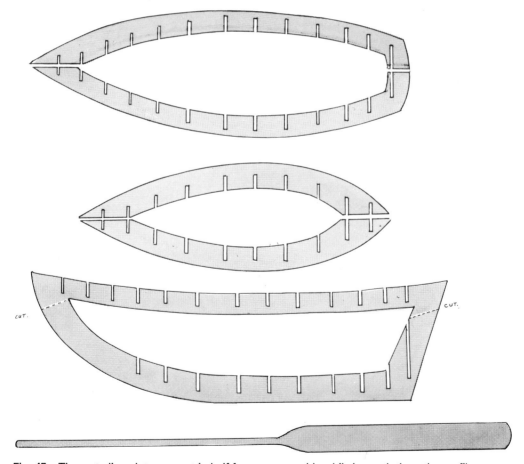

Fig. 45   The waterline plates are cut in half for easy assembly while beneath them the profile, which is also the backbone of the model, has two temporary cuts made for the same purpose. Below the profile is the stem and keel shoe plate which has to be carefully composed from a paper template.

Silhouette model in a frame

For those with a natural eye for line (which is a kind way of describing folk like myself who can't handle the technical side) this may present a more inviting project than the complications required for a genuine half model. It's a sort of flattened half model, halfway towards a painting. Indeed like a painting it permits the addition of masts and sails which, after all, are half the beauty of a sailing craft.

It is quite a simple model to make because instead of all the bits of paper and string hung delicately in the air as they would be in a ship in a bottle, they are, with this model, each stuck down securely on a sheet of glass. I have seen similar models where hessian or felt is used as the back cloth but apart from the difficulty of glueing small items to felt or hessian (and the problems of removing the glue stains if you make a mistake) neither of these materials has the reflective quality of glass which also enhances the three dimensional effect. The back of the glass is painted.

There isn't very much to say about the construction of this model which has not already been covered in the item about making a ship in a bottle. The separate parts of hull, rigging, masts, booms and gaffs etc. are painted and varnished before sticking down on the glass and the sails, which are painted with emulsion, are made to billow with the help of a little plasticine – a model like this allows quite a lot of cheating. A final word about the frame. This must be a deep, protrusive moulding (in this case a standard pattern bought from a hardware shop) so that the model appears to sit within it. A full bodied model in a flat frame looks, well, precarious.

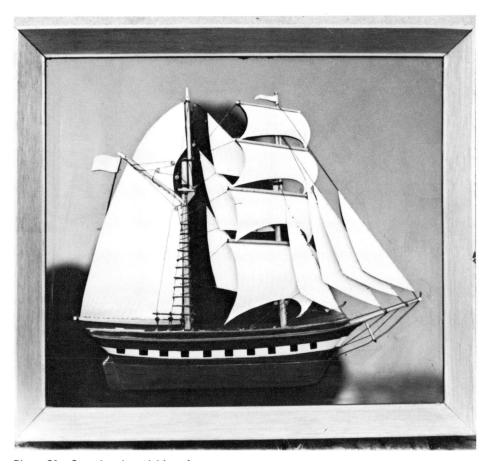

Photo 20   Completed model in a frame.

A sailing man's wind vane

This idea comes from a book written many years ago by Hervey Garrett Smith who in turn got it from his grandfather's outdoor privy – apparently the old man had the thing rigged up on the roof. The boats were shaped from blocks of softwood but the list of other materials used in the construction makes quaint reading today: 'Arms and masts made of oak, sails cut from a sheet of zinc . . .' Almost certainly today's handyman could make a far more efficient and durable job with aluminium, Tufnel bearings, plastic extrusion, etc.

It's a very esoteric wind vane and only a man who understands sailing can figure out what is going on. Each boat in turn luffs up, goes about, pays off, broad reaches and finally gybes and, unless you understand the significance of all that, I suppose the model just seems to be going round and round.

Incidentally, the mainsheet, which is made of chain to obviate chafe, is set to allow the sail to swing out to a maximum of 40 degrees either way.

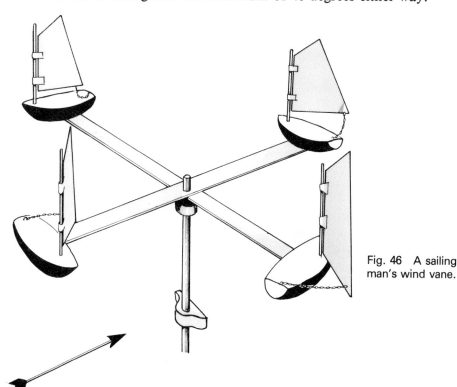

Fig. 46 A sailing man's wind vane.

DECORATIVE

Coachwhipping and other ornamental covers

Much of today's so-called 'fancywork' had, in its original form, an important work-a-day purpose. Coachwhipping is a perfect example of this and even now it performs a function unrivalled by all the glittering extrusions of the plastics industry. Take my spiral staircase. For fifty years it stood in the rain at the back of our local cinema where it performed an unseen but nonetheless stalwart job as a fire escape. Then one day they tore it down and the scene of so many boyhood adventures, from Snow White to Mildred Wilkins, ended up a heap of rubble and corkscrewed metal. All, that is, but the fire escape, which was spared from destruction and carted away to my home; well, it had been a part of my heritage! We covered the iron stair treads with carpet but the handrail, a sharp and nasty, twisting thing, presented much more of a problem. Then I remembered how we used to cover the handrails in the ships I had sailed in. Coachwhipping! (I suppose you were wondering when I was going to get round to it?)

Needless to add it transformed that rail into a perfect handgrip, comfortable to touch, non-slippery and very nice-looking. I gave it a couple of coats of white paint along with the stays, centre column and other parts and it melted in with its background beautifully. In fact that was the trouble, it was so anonymous that nobody ever noticed it, and that is why I'm making such a big thing of it here.

Of course you don't have to use canvas as I did. Coachwhipping can be done just as well with a cord or thin line and the sequence is exactly the same. It is usual however to stick to the same six strands since this seems to be about the maximum the human arms can cope with. However, each one of these six strands can comprise several parts or lines. Coachwhipping ought to be topped and tailed with a Turk's head and, since it is probably going to get dirty in everyday use, finished with a couple of coats of paint.

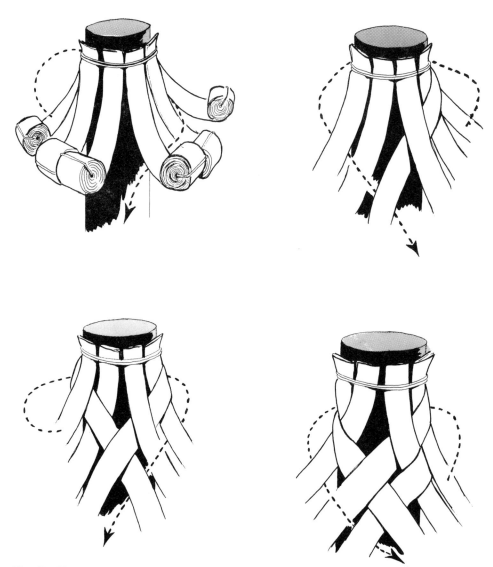

Fig. 47 Where large areas are to be covered, such as rails or mast pillars, coachwipping with canvas gets the job done quickly and suffers nothing in appearance. Start by cutting the canvas into strips, the longer the better, then fold them so that the cut edges are tucked inside the folds. The width of each strip must be slightly more than one-sixth of the circumference of the object being covered. Lay the strips on a table and, when satisfied that they look reasonably straight and parallel, run the back edge of a knife or similar tool over the folds; this presses them into a permanent crease. Roll up each strip and tie it as the drawing shows – not too tightly because the coil must be free to revolve. Seize the strips temporarily in place and begin the under-and-over sequence as described by the drawings. If you have to make joins then these will have to come underneath the overlapping pieces; wherever possible try to stagger them.

Half-hitching

Half-hitching or, as it is sometimes called, *needle hitching* is an ideal cover for tool handles, especially deck knives and potato peelers where it provides a sure grip in what are often wet and slippery conditions. It also has a decorative role. There is nothing of otherwise general interest I can say about half-hitching except to recommend its simple, unobtrusive construction to reluctant opera-goers.

Start by tucking or twisting a small eye in the end and pass the threaded needle through it. Pulled tight this forms the first loop and the first row of half-hitches are made around it. When this row is complete — take care to keep the work open and loose — start the second row by passing the needle under the loops left between the hitches. If the object is tapered then drop a stitch to accommodate the shrinking pattern.

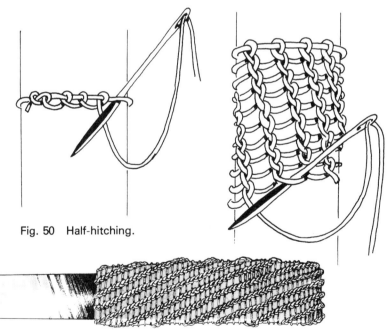

Fig. 48 Completed coachwhipping.

Fig. 50 Half-hitching.

Fig. 49 Half-hitching used on a knife handle. Although primarily used in a decorative role, half-hitching has very practical applications, such as the provision of a safe grip on a sharp galley or deck knife.

75

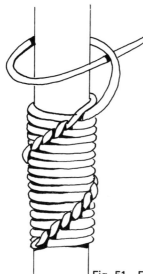

French Hitching

There is nothing very clever about French hitching; it is simply a row of half-hitches passed around an object. It is a very quick method of applying a cover that provides a good grip.

Fig. 51   French hitching.

Fender Hitching

This is very similar to needle hitching except that the hitch is passed behind the 'rib' instead of under the loop. Unlike the needle hitch the 'ribs' run straight down the object instead of spiralling. It is probably a smarter job than the former but care must be exercised to ensure that the ribs are kept straight.

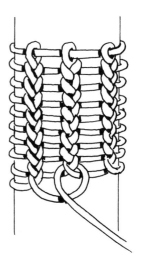

Fig. 52   Fender hitching.

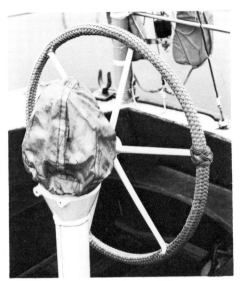

Photos 21 and 22 Two different examples of ornamental covering used for the same purpose. Photo 21 shows a complicated form of coachwhipping which includes eight strands of two part line while Photo 22 shows the very much quicker French hitching. Both examples have a comfortable feel about them.

Photo 23 French hitching used on a tiller.

Rope handles and toggles

Fig. 53 Continuous wall knot sennit.

Far be it from me to guess what you might need a little toggle for, my interest stops with the suggestion of how to make one. Certainly the opportunities are legion, you could make a fancy bell rope, a shackle pin lanyard, a door knocker, a suitcase handle, a hanging strap, heaps of different things. Probably the easiest sennits to make (sennit is the name given to this kind of fancywork) are those which incorporate the wall and crown knots. We have used these knots several times throughout the book and their construction should now be familiar. To begin, why not try the continuous wall sennit? This is merely a series of wall knots, one on top of the other, made with four separate strands of cord initially seized together. Four cords are used because this gives the sennit a square shape and that, since it is an unusual way to present rope, is uniquely attractive.

Alternatively you could make a series of simple crown knots and end up with a still neater finish. Even more so if you were to alternate the crown knots, which is to say make one crown knot by passing the strands to the right and the next one with the strands tucked to left, and so on.

The square sennit may look familiar, it is the knotting used for stern gland packing where its regular square shape provides a good watertight seal on the propeller shaft and parts inside the stuffing box. It consists of eight strands which are first seized together and then divided into two groups. The strand on the extreme left is passed behind, and then taken under and over pairs of strands on the right. The strand on the extreme right is passed behind and under and over pairs in the left hand group. The process is repeated over again using the extreme right and left strands in each case. My dog has a lead made with a square sennit and he is very proud of it.

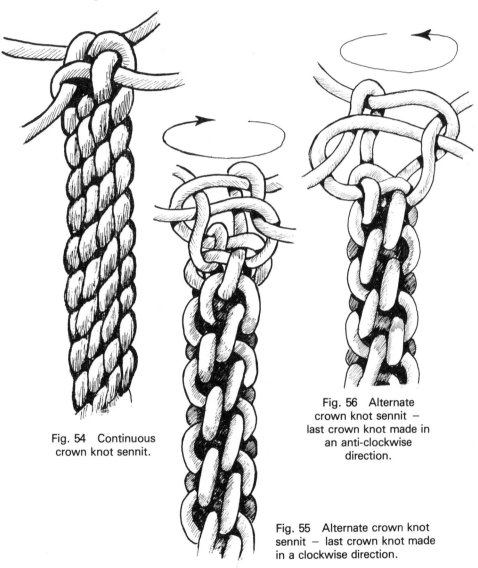

Fig. 54 Continuous crown knot sennit.

Fig. 56 Alternate crown knot sennit — last crown knot made in an anti-clockwise direction.

Fig. 55 Alternate crown knot sennit — last crown knot made in a clockwise direction.

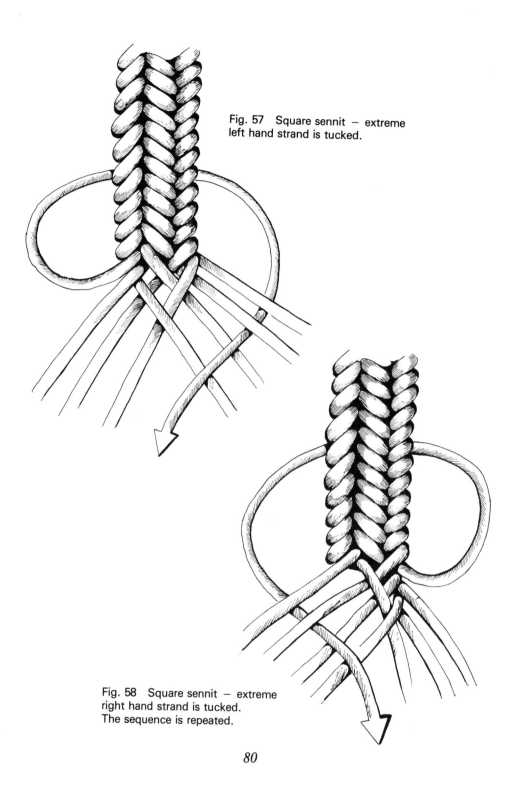

Fig. 57 Square sennit — extreme
left hand strand is tucked.

Fig. 58 Square sennit — extreme
right hand strand is tucked.
The sequence is repeated.

Photo 24   Alternate crown sennit used as a shackle pull.

Laminated chart table top

A simple idea, but one which is quite practical, is to laminate the chart you most often use to the top of your chart table. Not only does it make a welcome relief from the commonplace but means that the area you regularly

Fig.59   A local chart laminated onto the top of the chart table as a practical decoration.

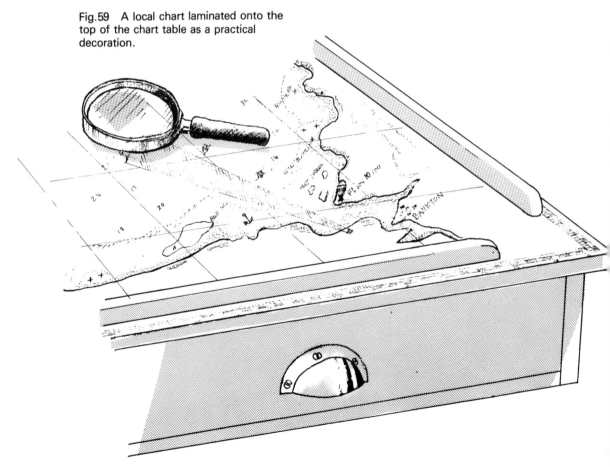

cruise is permanently on display and preserved under several coats of varnish. It doesn't have to be the complete chart, indeed it could be a composite of the harbours and bays you most frequently visit. Begin by sanding the top of the chart table with a fine paper until you have an almost perfectly smooth finish, then take a new chart and cut out the part which you are most likely to use (or sections patterned together as you choose) and lay it over the chart table to check for size. It is recommended that you take the chart right out to the edge even if this means temporarily removing the fiddle rails. Use a good quality adhesive and once this has been evenly applied, lay the chart down carefully from one corner smoothing the job with one hand to release the air bubbles. Once the glue is thoroughly dry, and you may like to leave it a few hours, apply the first satin finish or matt varnish (a high gloss throws up too many reflections). At least three coats of varnish are needed and sand well with fine paper between applications. Because of the wide variety of glues, clear laquers, fixatives, varnishes and sealants available, it is wise to experiment first with the materials you have chosen before finally committing them to the chart.

Decorative nameboards and such

Carving, gilt work and ornamentation in wood have been as much a part of wooden craft as the sails on the masts which drove them. Reasons for their origin are long forgotten but quite likely derived from superstition when the various 'lucky' items such as fish eyes, rabbits' feet and sharks' fins began to go off in warm weather and a more durable imitation was agreed upon. Certainly it was something like that which prompted the introduction of

Photo 25

Photo 26

bare-breasted figureheads. Long held that a naked woman could calm the seas, the wooden stand-in probably started because some fish wife somewhere, hanging out the washing or painting her fence, finally got fed up with whipping up her vest each time her old man went out fishing. Still, whatever the reasons this whim of the seaman to ornament his ship is wholly international, for no matter what part of the globe you go to you will find fishing boats and working craft with carved or coloured embellishments. The 'eye' on the bow is a typical example. For centuries fishermen have painted the big Muppet-like eye on the bow to help the boat 'see' where it is going. It is a practice you will find all around the Mediterranean, the Arab countries and even in China, except there perhaps a slightly more almond-shaped version.

In Europe the ornamentation peak was reached in the middle of the 18th century when the intricate scroll work around the stern, or 'gingerbread' as it is known, came to reach such an unreasonable proportion of the building costs that the Royal Navy banned its use in ships altogether. Of course it

Photos 27 and 28

came creeping back, just the same as it is creeping back in small boats today; ornamentation in wood it seems is a feature of the sailor's art that simply refuses to die.

One suggestion is to decorate your ship with a carved nameboard (Photos 27 and 28). Letter carving is surprisingly easy to do and although special gouges (curved chisels) are recommended, it is perfectly possible to manage with ordinary mortice chisels. As Photo 27 suggests, this example was made with them. The two important considerations are the style and spacing of the letters which is best found by experimentation. For style it is a good idea to search the advertisements in magazines; advertisers can use very attractive typefaces. Find one you like, scale it up and draw the outline straight onto the wood. It is important to keep chisel edges razor sharp or the shape of the letters will suffer. Try also to maintain the same angle of cut and keep the angle shallow. Use the smaller chisels for serifs and cutting around corners. The letters can be finished with a yellow paint or gold leaf inlay or, as in this case, simply varnish. The board looks good on bulwarks, cockpit or cabin sides.

The disadvantage of nameboards on the boat's side is the fact that you have to make *two* of them, unless of course you adopt a one-sided approach like the mate I knew who only painted that side of the ship that faced the owner's riverside office. Transom nameboards on the other hand are a one-off job so you can afford to be a little more enterprising and perhaps have a go at the decorative scroll boards as shown in Figures 60 and 61.

Fig. 60   The traditional colour for the banner is blue — pale, almost white, behind the letters but darkening to a deep shade at the ends to emphasise the third dimension suggested by the folds. The banner is customarily edged with gold or darkened yellow and the letters are painted.

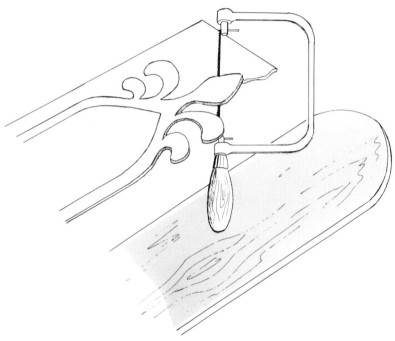

Fig. 61 This more decorative variety can either be carved entirely from a length of hardwood or you can cheat and make it in relief as the drawing shows. Cut the ornate part from a piece of plywood, chamfer the edges slightly and glue to a backing piece of different colour or darker shade.

Signwriting too is less difficult than it looks and success lies in having the right tools for the job. Most important are good quality sable brushes. Also required are a quantity of white spirit, a small pallet for loading the brush, a piece of chalk with a sharpened edge, pencils, compasses for drawing curves and a steadying stick or mahl which is padded and covered in chamois leather. Any marine paint can be used but it does need to be well strained. Spacing is important just as much as dexterity with the brush. It cannot be measured, it can only be done by eye. The letters W and I are the most tricky and if placed together must not encroach on each other's space. Curved letters require more space each side than straight ones, letters such as W, V and A can encroach on each other's space and the letter I needs proportionally more space to make it stand out and especially when placed next to a curved letter. Self contained letters like J, L and F can generally be placed nearer to their neighbours. Horizontal lines should be drawn thinner than vertical ones.

Fig. 62 Something for the wood carver to set his teeth into is this traditional scroll work typically found on trailboards either side of the bow. However there is no compulsion to position it here; an item like this stands well on its own and could be used as ornamentation in many places throughout the boat, both inside and out.

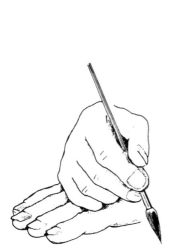

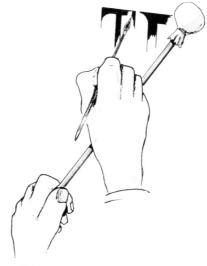

Fig. 63 Signwriters' paint brushes or 'pencils' are held like a pen with the forefinger on top. This enables the brush to be rolled when making corners and keeps the point down on the surface and the curve to be made in one sweep. Practice using the pencil by resting the working hand on top of the other.

Fig. 64 The mahl or resting stick is essential to hold the hand steady. Start by making chalk dots at the strategic points of each letter then use the brush to join up. This is better than trying to draw the entire outline of the letter when effort is concentrated on keeping the brush on the line instead of making a bold and independent stroke.

Fig. 65   Apart from nameboards, notices, sail numbers on the dodgers and deck, the boat's name on the lifebuoys makes a tiddly job. Gold leaf is the preferred material for letters with black to define the edges. Space the letters out evenly each side from the centre.

Turk's head

Almost every item of decorative work aboard a boat seems to begin or end with a Turk's head, partly because it is so adaptable but more probably because it is the one fancy knot which everyone can remember. It is said that the Turk's head was originally tied around footropes beneath the yards to improve the sailor's footing while handling sails, but there are at least a hundred variations and it is difficult to be sure where or when it was first used. It probably had many different applications. In a boat it makes a good fender each end of a sheet horse, it can be used to mark the 'midship' position on a wheel, as an anti-chafe guard around a spinnaker pole, or in a purely decorative role.

START WITH
FIGURE OF 8.

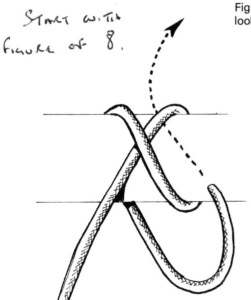

Fig. 66a   Any material can be used but braided line looks best. Keep work loose to begin with.

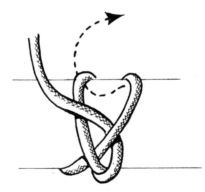

Fig. 66b   Complete the first round, turn and tuck as shown, then at this stage pass the bight on the right hand side beneath the bight on the left so that a loop is formed.

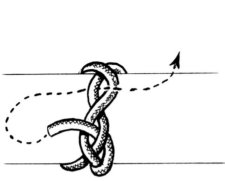

Fig. 66c   Pass the working end through the loop making sure to observe the strict under and over sequence.

Fig. 66d   A little confusing at first sight but all that has happened is that the working end has been passed under the bight on the right. Its position can be compared to the bottom of Fig. 66e.

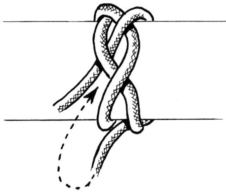

Fig. 66e   The back of the knot or what you would see if you were to rotate the knot 180 degrees. (If the spar, post or whatever is large in diameter you might wish to increase the number of scallops in which case you repeat the operation shown in Figures 66c and 66d). At this stage the basic construction is finished and doubling or tripling of the turns begins.

Fig. 66f   The working end is shown at the start of the doubling process which is a logical following round. When sufficient turns have been put in, work out the slack to get the knot as tight as possible and secure and hide the ends underneath. Turk's heads look better when painted.

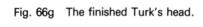

Fig. 66g   The finished Turk's head.

CANVAS WORK

A sea bag

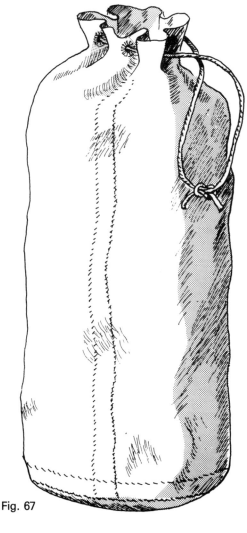

Fig. 67

Three things guaranteed the new deck boy a noisy reception; a tin trunk, hob nail boots and a need to keep scratching himself. In the confines of a small vessel, all three were highly anti-social. Top of the list were the boots and the termites, but as soon as these had been dispatched he would be given a piece of canvas with which to make a sea bag (Fig. 67). A sea bag is the simplest form of bag with the rather special considerations that it neither rattles nor bangs nor takes up space when empty. Also important, so far as the first trip deck boy was concerned, was that its construction included all the various forms of canvas work. While duck canvas is the best to use, a heavier grade is quite acceptable, although it's harder to sew. Size can be tailored to suit your own needs but something like a depth of 3 ft with a diameter of 15 ins is usual (if the opening is too narrow it is difficult to hunt things inside). Start by cutting out the main panel, which will need to be several inches bigger than the finished size to allow for the seams. The two long edges are overlapped and joined with a flat seam as described in Fig. 68b. It helps if you draw a pencil line where the stitches will run and press the back of a knife blade over the folds to give them a permanent crease. Canvas is hard to sew and you will need a palm to push the needle through the three thicknesses. You also need a special waxed thread called sail twine and a No. 16 sail needle. The neatness of the stitches is all important. Nothing looks nicer than a line of perfect stitches; nothing looks worse than 'Homeward bounders'. To repeat, the stitching is hard work and it is necessary to anchor the canvas against the pull of the needle. The usual way to do this is to lay the seam across your lap and as work progresses tuck the completed part under one leg. Alternatively secure the end of the seam to some strong point by means of a line and sail hook driven through the canvas. Use double thread and instead of a knot to secure the end leave a few inches of thread and tuck this along the seam and sew round it. About five stitches to the inch is usual for duck canvas and it is most important always to thread (pass) the needle at the same angle. To make a join, unpick the last half stitch and pass the new thread through the hole left by the unpicked stitch. Now cut both old and new thread so they each have about 1½ ins of end, twist them together and lay them under the seam where progressive stitches will hold them in position. There is a risk when sewing canvas that one edge will hunch up to produce an uneven and unsightly finish. This can be prevented if the work is held with a number of tacking stitches (say one every 6 in or so) put along the seam beforehand. Alternatively the seam can be held in position with sail needles.

The top of the bag also has a flat seam but since it has to accommodate eyelets it will need to be rather deeper than the main seam. The eyelets can either be the manufactured brass variety or they can be sewn in. Sewn stitches look more professional and save having to borrow or buy the right sized punch and die.

The diagrams explain how the bottom panel is attached although note that in this instance the preliminary 'tacking' stitches are vital. It isn't necessary however to use a flat seam. I have made several bags by turning the work inside out and putting in a simple round seam; however, a flat seam is stronger.

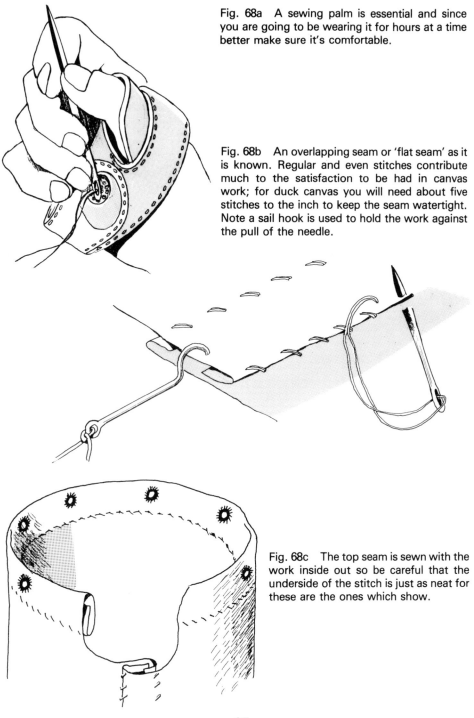

Fig. 68a   A sewing palm is essential and since you are going to be wearing it for hours at a time better make sure it's comfortable.

Fig. 68b   An overlapping seam or 'flat seam' as it is known. Regular and even stitches contribute much to the satisfaction to be had in canvas work; for duck canvas you will need about five stitches to the inch to keep the seam watertight. Note a sail hook is used to hold the work against the pull of the needle.

Fig. 68c   The top seam is sewn with the work inside out so be careful that the underside of the stitch is just as neat for these are the ones which show.

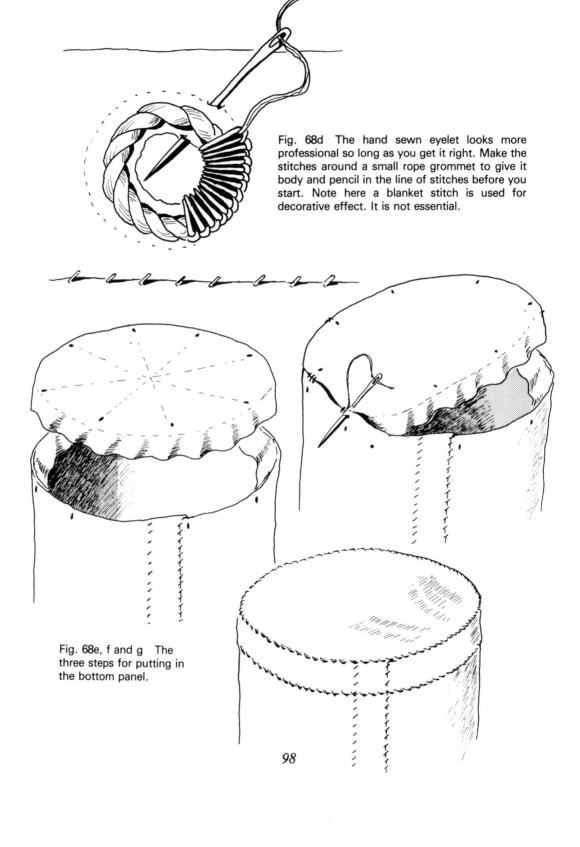

Fig. 68d The hand sewn eyelet looks more professional so long as you get it right. Make the stitches around a small rope grommet to give it body and pencil in the line of stitches before you start. Note here a blanket stitch is used for decorative effect. It is not essential.

Fig. 68e, f and g The three steps for putting in the bottom panel.

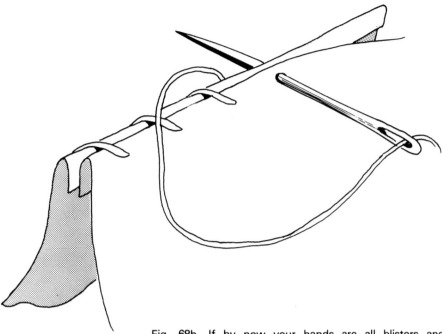

Fig. 68h If by now your hands are all blisters and callouses you may prefer to use the optional 'round seam' for putting in the bottom panel. (You only have to sew round once). The round seam is put in with the bag turned inside out and the stitches should be practically invisible from the outside.

A ditty bag

Fig. 69

'Ditty' is a euphemism, it ought to be called a *handbag*, for that virtually was what it was. A bag to contain the sailor's personal bits and pieces which, when not carried about, lived on a nail near his bunk. Nowadays ditty bags are larger and more often used for shopping, vegetables or carrying the batteries ashore, but even those mundane chores needn't preclude the decoration which, size apart, separates it so clearly from the sea bag. The fancy work is mainly contained in the draw strings, although sewn-in initials and tassels were not unknown. Three doubled cords are seized in the middle to form an eye and around this eye a blanket stitch is sewn. This drawing doesn't show it but if you have mastered some of the examples in *Rope handles and toggles* then you may wish to incorporate a few inches of sennit work before splaying out the ends to form the draw strings. A Turk's head which slides up and down is used to close the bag.

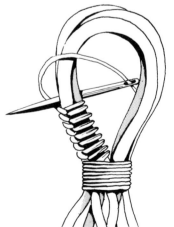

Fig. 70 To make an eye serve the mid parts together and dress with blanket stitching.

100

A wind scoop

For all its weird appearance a canvas wind scoop makes a tremendous difference to life below decks in warm weather and the beauty of it is that it takes up so little space, collapsing like an opera hat when you let go the suspending halyard. Size can be varied according to need but proportions are roughly the same as the sea bag; construction is similar also. To keep the scoop wide open a couple of wire grommets are required. A wire grommet is made in similar manner to the rope grommet, i.e. from one long strand

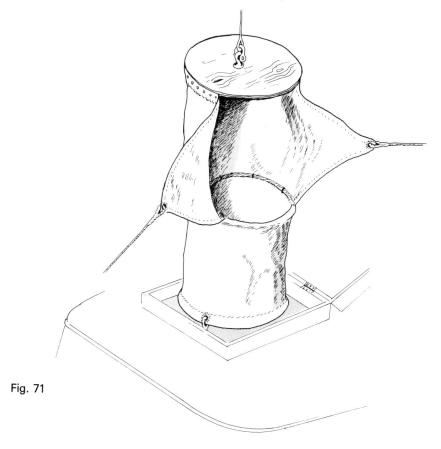

Fig. 71

fashioned into an overhand knot and re-laid in its suggested direction. The bottom grommet is sewn inside the seam and a couple of eyelets are worked in to hold the securing lines. The grommet beneath the mouth of the scoop is simply stitched to the canvas walls. A plywood disc is nailed in place at the top with its edges scored to ensure a good tight fit. The scoop is suspended from a halyard and held to the wind with guy lines.

Fig. 72 Two diagonals are cut into the wall of the bag to make the side flaps.

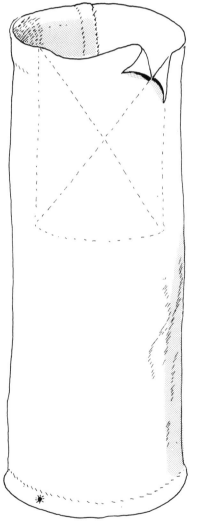

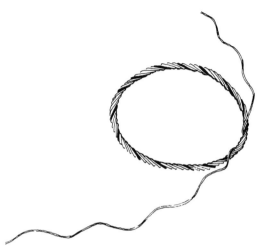

Fig. 73 The wire grommet is finished off with an overhand knot and the ends tucked a few times against the lay in the manner of a rope eye splice.

Fig. 74 A plywood disc forms the top of the scoop.

A canvas bucket

It hasn't the clatter of the galvanised pail, nor the perfidy of the plastic sort that leaves you grasping the handle and nothing else. This is the genuine, bedouin, sailor's bucket and aboard a boat it has no equal. Lightweight, tough, takes up no space − the only thing it cannot do is boil up your laundry on the galley stove. It is made with a No. 4 canvas and the approximate dimensions are 9 ins (230 mm) in diameter and 1 ft deep. Begin as if you were making a ditty bag with a flat seam down the side then sew a rope grommet in the bottom. Only the better class buckets have rope grommets which provide a comfortable base for it to sit on and gives you something to grip when emptying water from it. The canvas is turned in at the bottom to receive the rope. On top of the grommet a plywood disc is placed and this should be a snug fit. Cooper tacks are used to nail the disc in place and the centres should be fairly close to ensure a watertight join. Traditionally a wooden mast hoop was sewn inside the upper seam but if this proves a difficult acquisition then a wire grommet will have to be substituted.

Fig. 75

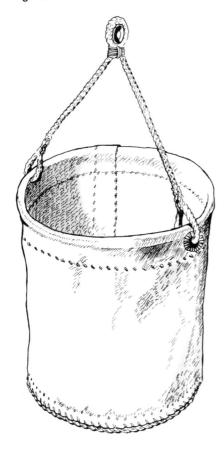

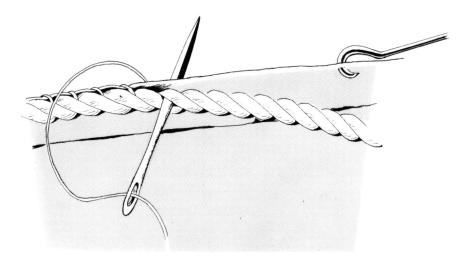

Fig. 76   A rope grommet is sewn inside the bottom and upon this rests the plywood base.

Photo 29   The completed canvas bucket.

FOR THE FUN OF IT

A submarine which dives

Sailing with small children − I mean the pure enjoyment of moving under sail − is the bit you squeeze in on the way to and from the beach, and even that can turn into a riot if they suspect you're dragging your heels. One way to deep them quiet is to trade on their infant delight at seeing the same silly joke repeated, which is undoubtedly why somebody invented this submarine. Towed behind the boat it will, if you slacken or tighten the tow line, dive and bob up to the surface, which is an exercise guaranteed to fascinate the mature adult for about twenty seconds, but on the other hand it'll keep the kids attention riveted right the way across the Atlantic.

You'll need a length of timber approximately 2 ft long, and to make things easy use softwood. Shape it as near to the shape of a submarine as you can get (or a simple cigar-shape will do). Build a conning tower on top while below, to keep it ballasted, screw on a piece of lead, or iron. Ballasting is important for the boat must float but only just.

Use a flat piece of tin such as a biscuit tin lid and cut out the shape of a rudder and two hydroplanes. (You can generally cut tin with an old pair of scissors.) Make a vertical saw cut in the stern and fix in the rudder. The hydroplanes are attached in the same way forward except of course that they are placed horizontally. Glue them in place with an epoxy resin adhesive.

Screw a cup hook into the bow of the boat and with a pair of pliers close up the 'eye'. This is the towing hook and a thin line several fathoms long is attached.

Paint the boat white or a very light grey so that it will show up under water and finally remember to secure the 'players' soundly to the aft pulpit; you know how kids tend to jump in the air whenever they get excited.

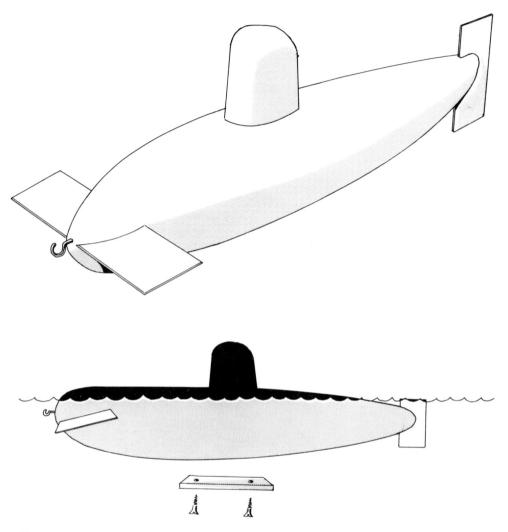

Fig. 77 a, b Hydroplanes, rudder and ballast arrangement.

A bespoke sailing cap

I was once in a ship seized by an epidemic of cap making. Some mad hatter started it off and the others, I suppose delighted to discover hat making involved no black art, simply followed in his wake. I have since reflected on why it should have taken off like it did and concluded that hats are an upward extension of one's personality, which is probably why we find it difficult to find one that really suits us. What better excuse then but to fashion a hat in the image one sees oneself – Breton fisherman or South American Admiral –

Fig. 78

so long as you can handle a pair of scissors and a needle. Favoured materials are blue denim, blue serge or duck canvas. Start with the rim which is simply a long rectangular shape folded several times to induce some sort of stiffness. The rim has to fit around your head so when this measurement is found mark and sew the ends together. The peak has to be banana-shaped, stitched and turned inside out; remember though to leave enough material to sew inside the rim. A piece of lino does for stiffening. The brim consists of a circular piece on top and four crescent-shaped pieces underneath. Once again these are stitched together and turned inside out before attaching to the brim.

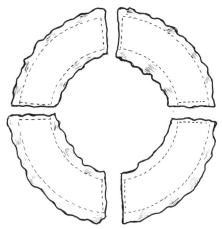

Fig. 79 Cut out a piece of material slightly larger than the brim.

Fig. 80 Four pieces to make the underside of the brim. Stitch together as indicated by the dotted lines, turn the work inside out and the brim should look as in Figure 81.

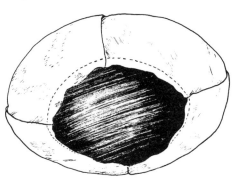

Fig. 81 Completed brim ready for sewing to the rim.

Fig. 82 The peak of the cap is sewn along the outer edge only and once again the work is turned inside out.

Fig. 83 Stiffener for the peak cut out of linoleum although the preferred material is engineroom gasket.

Fig. 84 The excess material at the top of the peak is tucked inside the folds of the rim and sewn in place.

Fig. 85 Decorate chinstay made from rope; optional extra, for South American Admirals.

Rope sole sandals

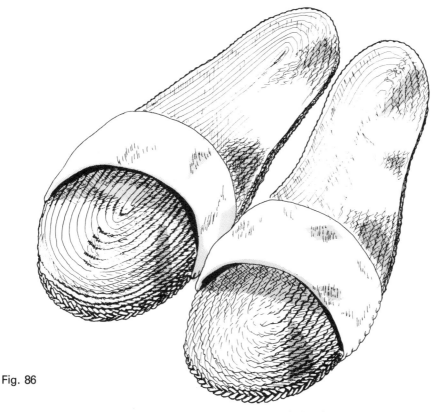

Fig. 86

Another of those everlasting jobs where the satisfaction comes, not so much from artistic achievement but the doggedness required to complete the damn thing.

You need a good length of, preferably, natural fibre rope which you then divide into yarns. Keep these yarns as long as possible for they have to be made up into a continuous length of 'flat sennit', which is the proper name for plaiting. You can however join new lengths on without too much difficulty. The plait is then formed to make the sole and stitched (and you will need a palm and sail needle to do this) through the top yarns only. The tops of the sandals are made from canvas, doubled over and stitched to the rope sole. Don't be put off by the time they take to make or what might appear to be a rather primitive finish. Rope soled shoes are long lasting, comfortable and have an enviably nautical look . . . sort of Robinson Crusoe-ish.

Fig. 87 Natural fibre rope is made up of three strands, each consisting of a dozen or so yarns. It is the yarns which you want, so cut them as long as practicable.

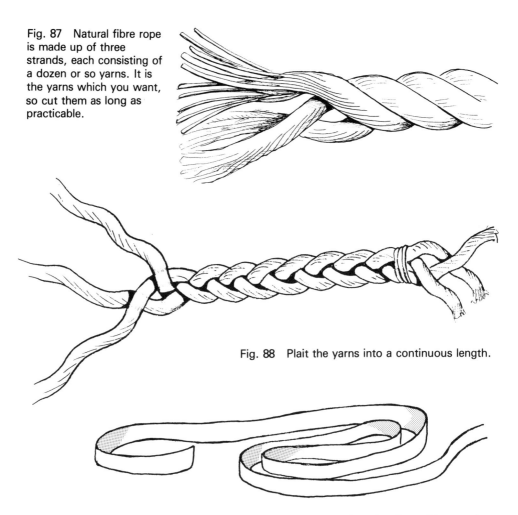

Fig. 88 Plait the yarns into a continuous length.

Fig. 89 The plait will have to be built up across the broad part of the foot by making a series of double runs.

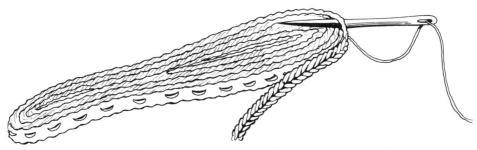

Fig. 90 Use a palm and needle and sew through the top yarn only.

112

Viewing bucket

(and another project)

Fig. 91

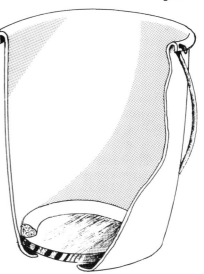

It is surprising how clearly you can see underwater once the surface ripples and reflections have been removed. The best way to do this is with a glass bottommed box well immersed. The observer, with his head tucked inside, can then look down and study his feet. It is for children of course, they will be quite happily employed for hours scouring along the sea bed. What I had in mind was something much more adult, a glass bottomed boat, but hadn't the courage to refer to it outright in the title. Just imagine the new world a glass bottomed boat would open up. You could study the fish, check on your anchor line and hunt out all the goodies other people have lost overboard. A small panel of toughened glass in the bottom of the boat would be all you would need (Fig. 91), suitably bedded with deep rubbing strakes on either side to protect it from damage and undue scratching when the boat is dragged up the beach. Inside you could place the bottom boards over it when not in use. (Perhaps for safety's sake the boat ought to be fitted with sufficient internal buoyancy to keep her afloat just in case the panel decides to leak.)

For the less courageous let's now return to the viewing bucket and 'cover' for the other suggestion (Fig. 92). Select a polythene bucket and cut out the bottom leaving a rim something like an inch wide. Next cut a circular disc of Perspex which exactly fits the bottom of the bucket and also buy a length of plastic beading to fit around the top edge. Degrease the sides of the bucket, where the Perspex will go, using white spirit or methylated spirit, then with coarse sandpaper roughen up the area and degrease again. Set the Perspex in a bed of epoxy resin glue, then spread the glue generously over the top edge of the Perspex and around the rim and press the plastic beading down on top.

Fig. 92

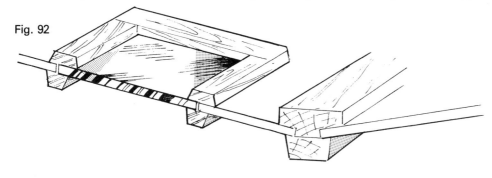

Dish swab

Photo 30

To be frank this brush, made out of old rope yarns and a piece of driftwood, is not the most efficient I have ever used, I can only conclude that it must be a strong peasant leaning within which makes me hang onto the thing. Either that or vanity, since visitors seem to admire it. Of course cooks have used rope brushes like this for washing up in the galley ever since ships went to sea, although I suppose that holds it responsible for the terrible standards of hygiene. Anyway, there it is, I don't necessarily commend it but come the day some guest empties your bowl containing a new nylon scrubber overboard, the old rope yarn brush would make a useful standby.

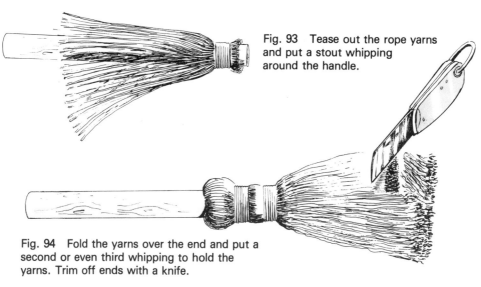

Fig. 93   Tease out the rope yarns and put a stout whipping around the handle.

Fig. 94   Fold the yarns over the end and put a second or even third whipping to hold the yarns. Trim off ends with a knife.

114

Table mats

Originally these were designed to cushion and quieten the blows of deck blocks. They were known very basely as *thump* mats or in Ireland *Tump* mats. If you have a sheet lead block which bangs against the deck and keeps you awake then this is the perfect answer; simply pass the shackle through the centre of the mat so that it looks like a choir boy's ruffle and then when the sheet slackens and the block falls the mat will be there to fender it.

However, a more delicate employment is to use it on the table where it is known, more delicately, as a *table* mat. Follow the drawings, tie loosely to begin with then when sufficient turns have been taken work out the slack. You will need to sew the turns of the scallops together to maintain a neat appearance (although I have seen this achieved in a simpler way by giving the entire mat a generous coat of lay-up resin). Its appearance will be improved and it will lie much flatter if it is given a good hammering with a wooden mallet, or if it is left squeezed in a vice overnight.

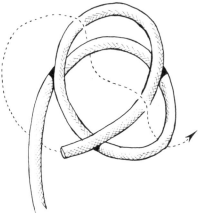

Fig. 95   The construction is begun the same as the companionway mat.

Fig. 96   The skeleton is finished and now begins the 'doubling' process. Pass as many turns as you wish but remember to follow the strict under-and-over sequence.

115

A knot board

This Christmas everybody gets a knot board. If you are another family that mass produces Christmas presents, then here is an item you can give to just about anyone of any age, of either sex, or whatever their interest; the only common thing they need is a nail and a wall to bang it in to. Constructing in bulk you need to keep things simple and like the boy in the English exam avoiding using the words he cannot spell, so you too avoid those knots which give you trouble. On the other hand if you plan to keep the thing or more to the point *sell* it − like the two crewmen in a Trinity House ship I served in who had commissions from pubs all over the West Country − then a more elaborate job is needed with the addition of name tabs beneath each knot for example.

Make the knots in white Terylene line. Cut through their ends with a hot knife to seal them and glue and stitch or pin them to a felt backcloth covering a piece of plywood. The knots can be displayed in an ordinary picture frame or, as shown here, on a circular board edged with a rope grommet.

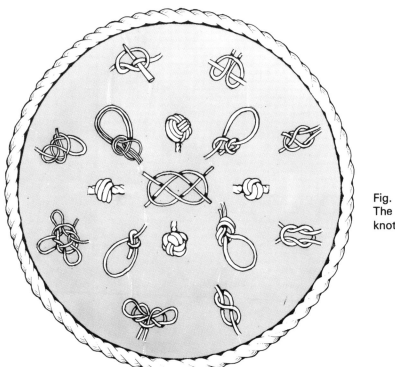

Fig. 97
The completed
knot board.

Chart lampshades

I am not going to make the hackneyed suggestion that this is a way to use up old charts, because nobody has *old charts* anymore — or rather we do, but they're dog-eared, crumpled, indecipherable and tea stained, fit only for navigation or lining your shoes. Better then to dig out an unused chart, preferably coloured, which covers some unlikely

Photo 32

part of the globe (although I understand that to sharp-eyed Finns, Sandskär is a pretty *important* unlikely part of the globe). The wire frame has to be purchased.

Panels are cut to fit the wire frame and varnished to look like parchment. Two coats should be sufficient, by which time the paper ought to have the luxurious, if not still damp, feel of the Dead Sea Scrolls. When dry the panels are stuck to the frame with an epoxy glue and/or stitched. If the shade is for a standard or table lamp and therefore large size, the stitch holes can be punched and sewed with coloured tape or rafia. Rope grommets top and bottom give the job a respectably nautical finish. (See *Wooden blocks* for instruction on making a grommet.)

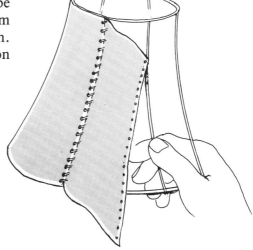

Fig. 98 The chart panels may be glued or sewn to the frame.

Rope cuff links

Now here is a change from vintage motor cars and blobs of Celtic art, a pair of cuff links with a wooden flag toggle to hold them and a decorative knot on top.

The knot employed here is the star knot which is intricate and tricky. You could however make a perfectly presentable pair of cuff links using either a wall and crown knot doubled or a double

Fig. 99

Matthew Walker (and not feel so mortified if you lost one), it's just that the troublesome star knot looks better. The toggle is made from a short length of dowel turned and shaped in the chuck of an electric drill held in the vice, and the toggle must of course be small enough to pass though the link hole in the cuff. Almost any kind of twine or small stuff can be used although a 1.5 mm diameter braided Terylene is probably the most attractive, particularly if you can find the coloured variety. The job is made more durable and better looking with a final coat of varnish, preferably nail varnish.

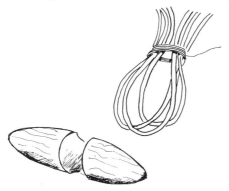

Fig 100 To make the five-stranded star knot, cut three lengths of line and bind them together over a short section in the middle with Terylene twine, to form an eye which will be fitted to the score carved in the wooden toggle.

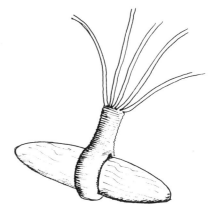

Fig. 101 Form an eye round the toggle using the bound section, and seize the two parts together. Finally, cut off one end to leave five strands.

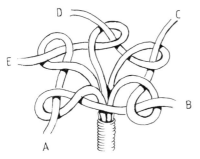

Fig. 102 The procedure in this drawing is impossible to describe in words. It is simply a matter of arranging each part as indicated remembering to maintain a strict rotation.

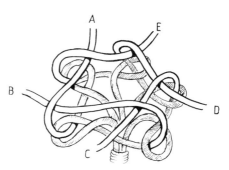

Fig. 103 Crown the ends to the left. It will help to retain a clear picture of what is going on if the ends are pulled reasonably tight and the knot kept in shape.

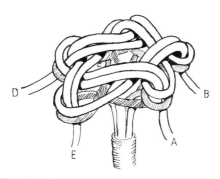

Fig. 104 Double the crowning process until the knot looks like this. If the strands are tight and tucking is difficult then use a large sail needle to 'thread' the tucks.

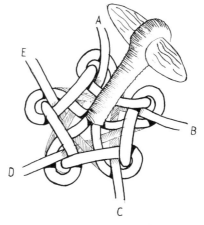

Fig. 105 Turn the work upside down and double the parts in the underside.

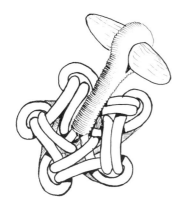

Fig. 106 The doubling process is complete and the ends should now emerge at the top of the knot, centred around the middle.

Fig. 107 The final tuck is made by passing the ends down through the centre to the underside of the knot where they are cut off. The varnish will help seal them in position.

Lee-Ho the lion

Photo 33

Lee-Ho the lion didn't turn out to be as fierce as he was supposed to be, in fact for a 'king of the jungle' he looks more like a rumpled hamster. I guess old rope and royalty are not compatible.

Begin with a short length of three-stranded rope and make a crown knot in the end (Fig. 108). Splice the three strands into the rope to form a back splice; this becomes the body. Cut off the surplus ends close to the end of the splice and pass a whipping around. Unlay the rope to the whipping and make a wall knot which is followed twice around to become the head (Fig. 109). Two ends are cut short to make the ears and the third is tucked out of sight.

You'll need some smaller rope for the legs. These have a single wall knot in the ends to make his paws. The legs are worked into the body with a fid and be sure to get them all the same length, although it is an interesting fact that I found a three legged lion stood more firmly than his quadruped buddy.

The lion's mane is made with bag-o-wrinkle which consists of lengths of rope yarn knotted to a double line of sail twine (Fig. 110). Get it as tight as you can and then cut off the ends to an equal length. Leave a good length of sail twine at each end and knot them together around the lion's neck.

The tail is made of small stuff teased out at the end, while the whiskers are simply rope yarns. The eyes in this case are drawing pins pressed into the rope with their heads painted, although small tacks look just as good. When the lion is complete give him a coat of varnish which will make his coat shine and his whiskers bristle. All lions are supposed to *bristle*.

Photo 34 *Lee-Ho*'s separate parts ready for assembly.

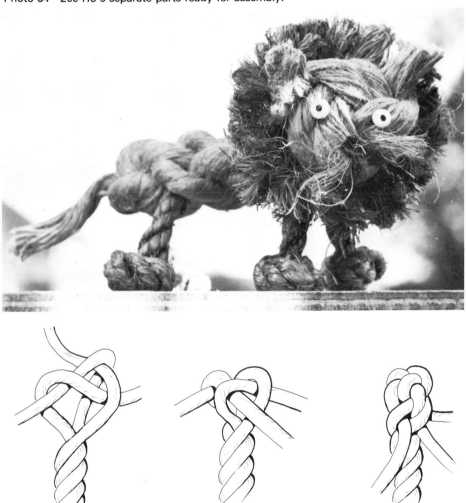

Fig. 108 His main trunk comprises a back splice which is begun with a crown knot to represent his parson's nose.

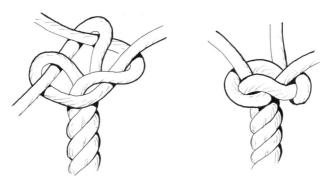

Fig. 109   Make a wall knot with the main trunk ends then follow this twice around, making it into a double wall knot to form the head.

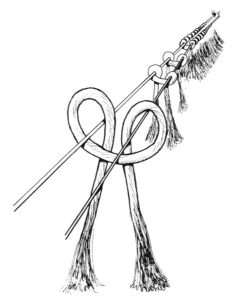

Fig. 110   Bag-o-wrinkle to form his mane.